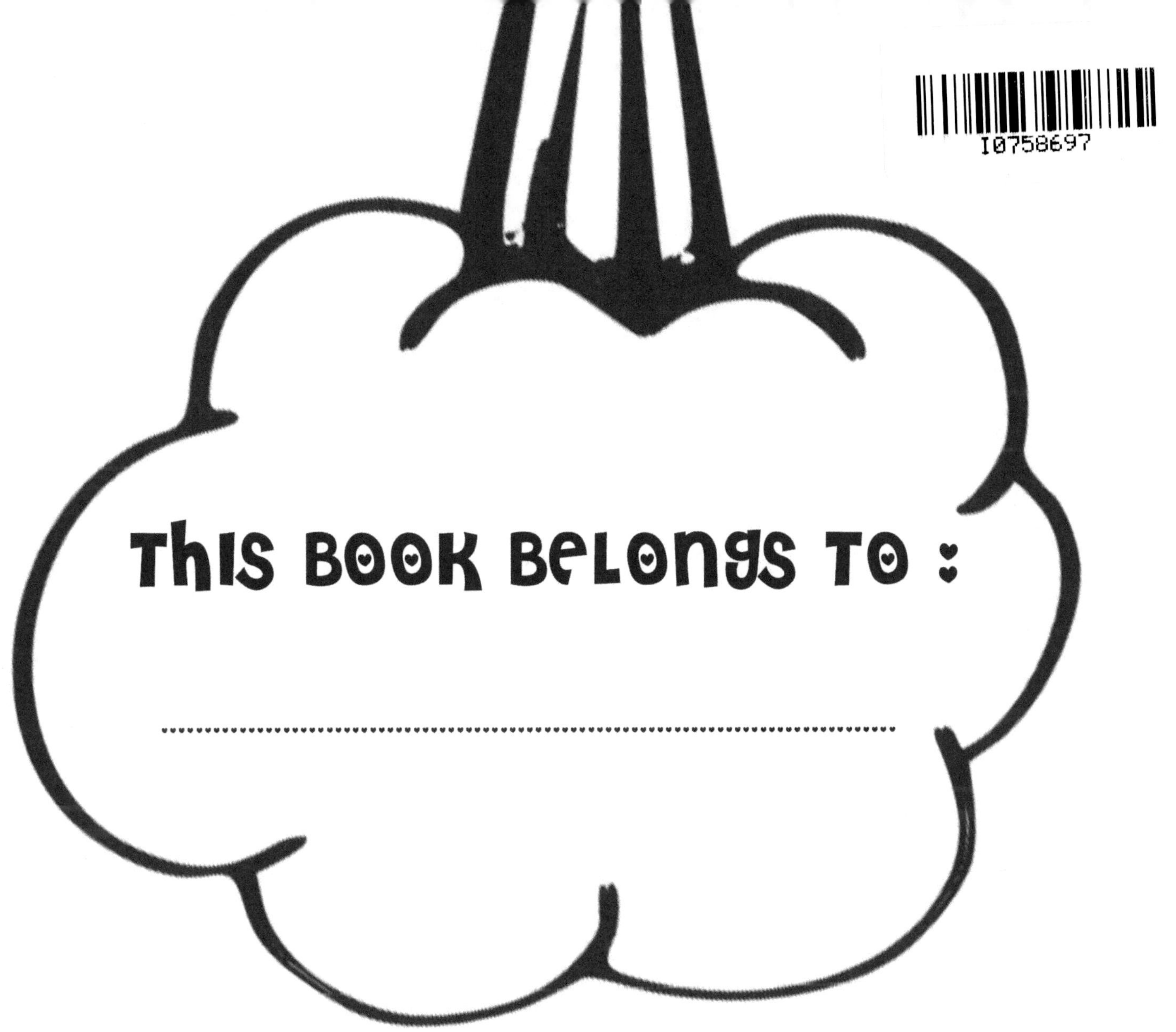

WARNING !

THE SMELL WON'T BE GOOD INSIDE

have A good
FARTING !

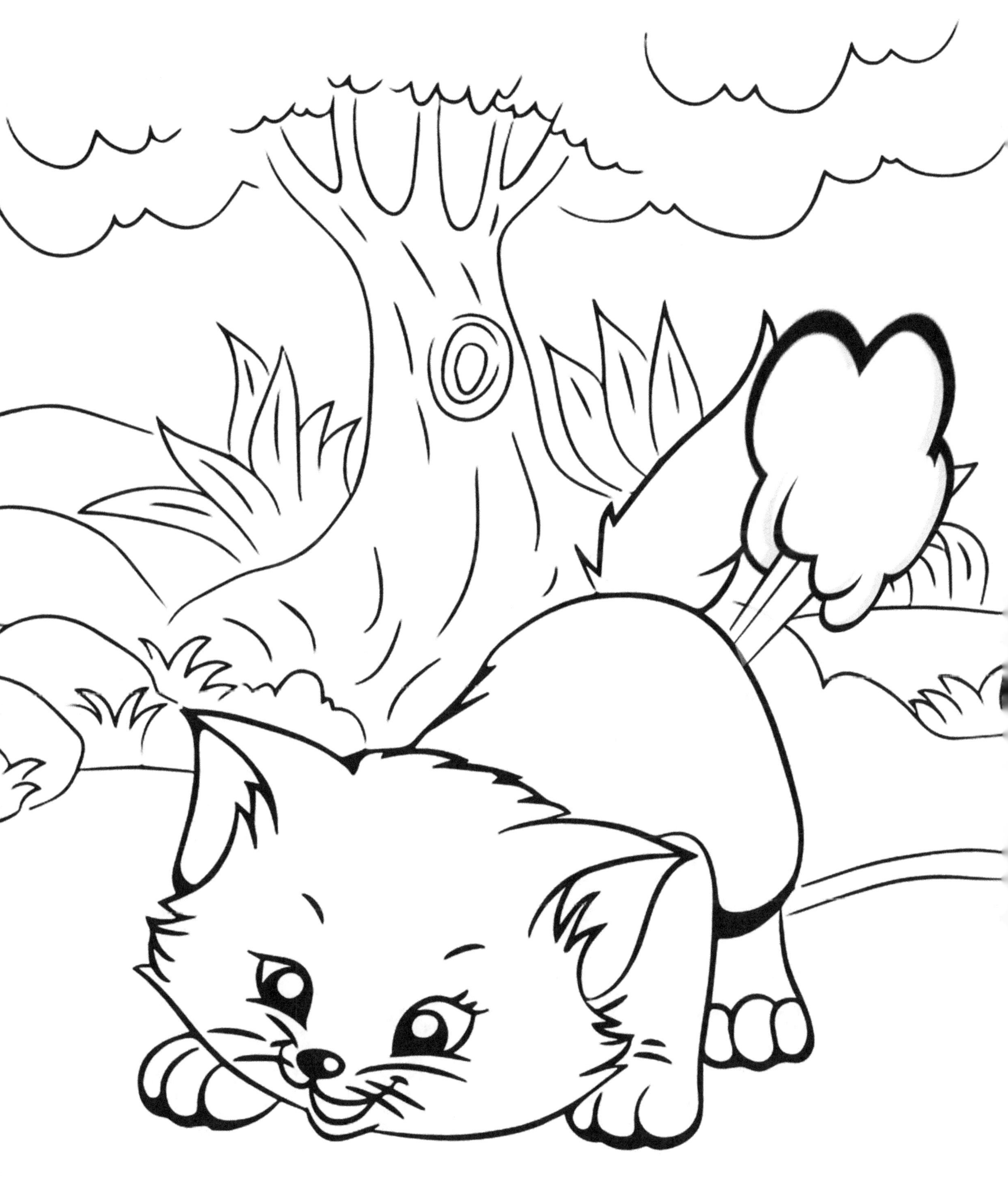

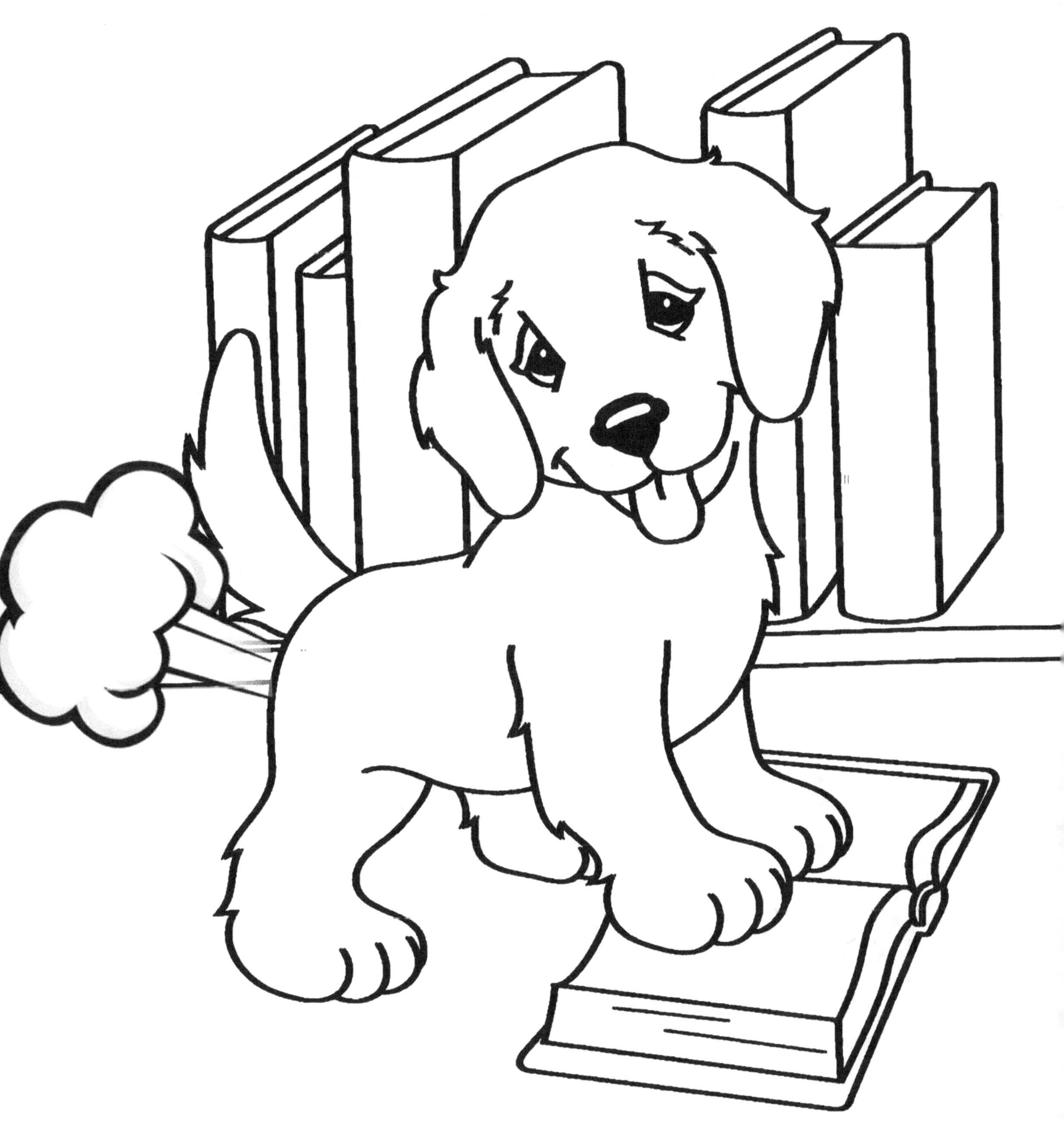

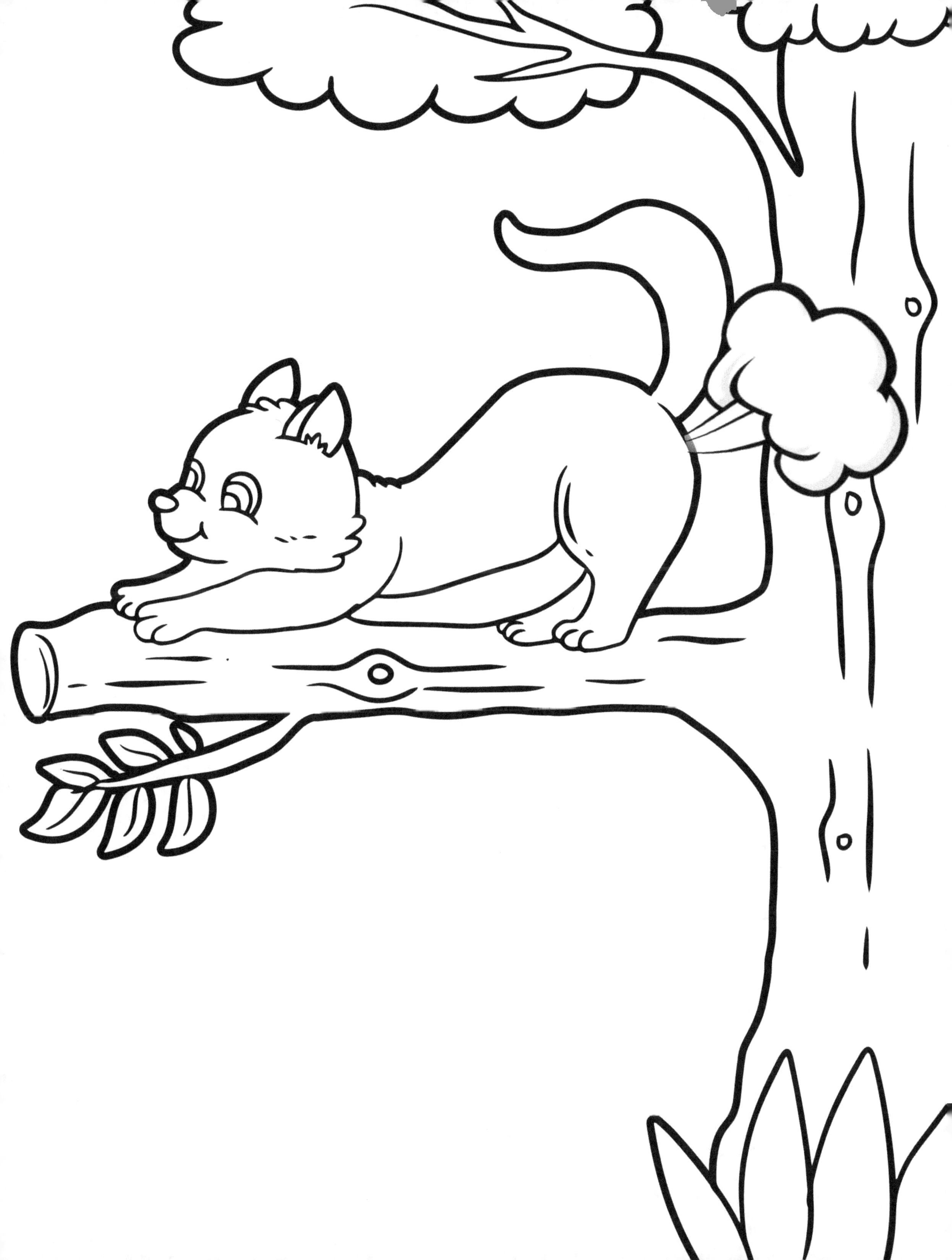

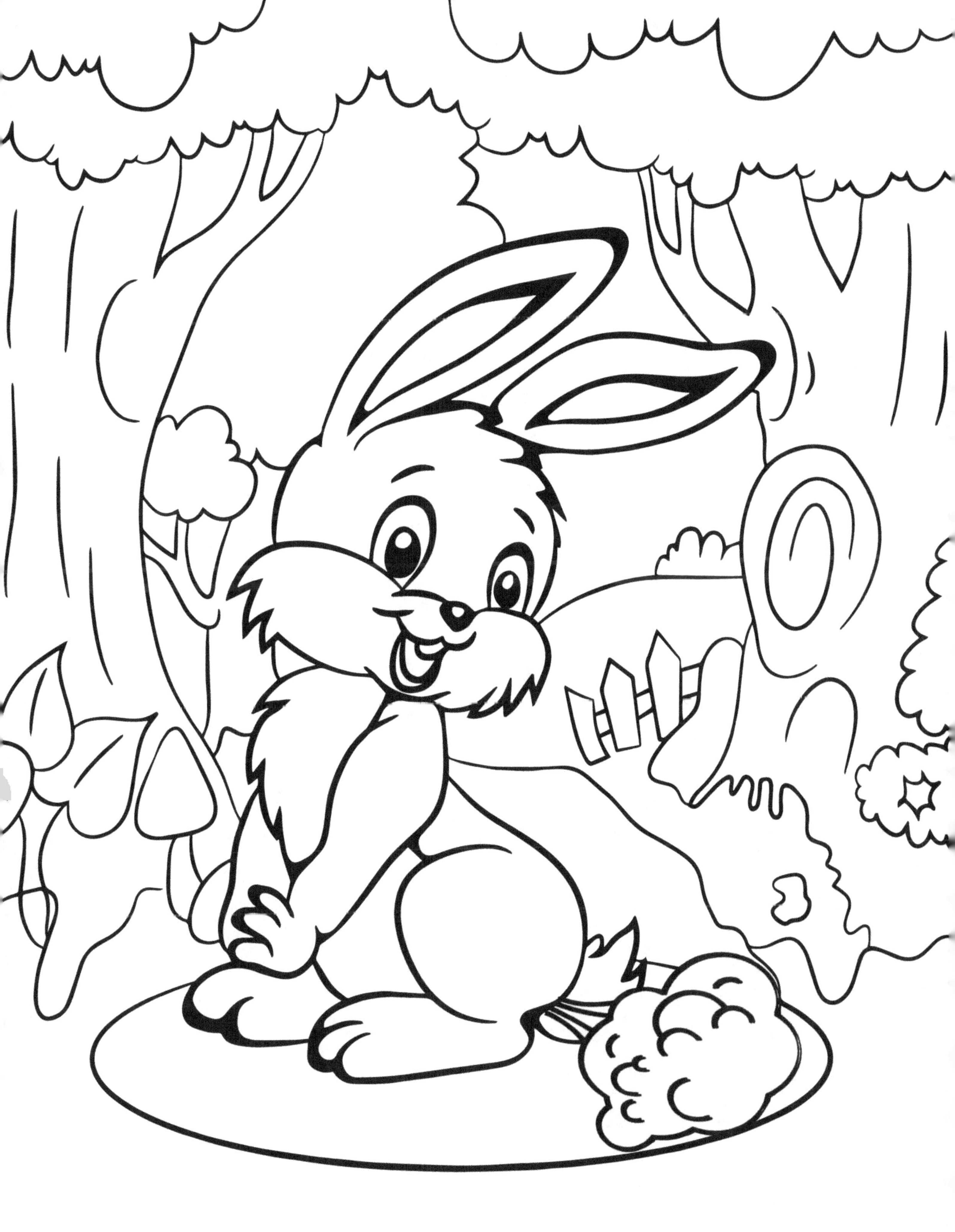

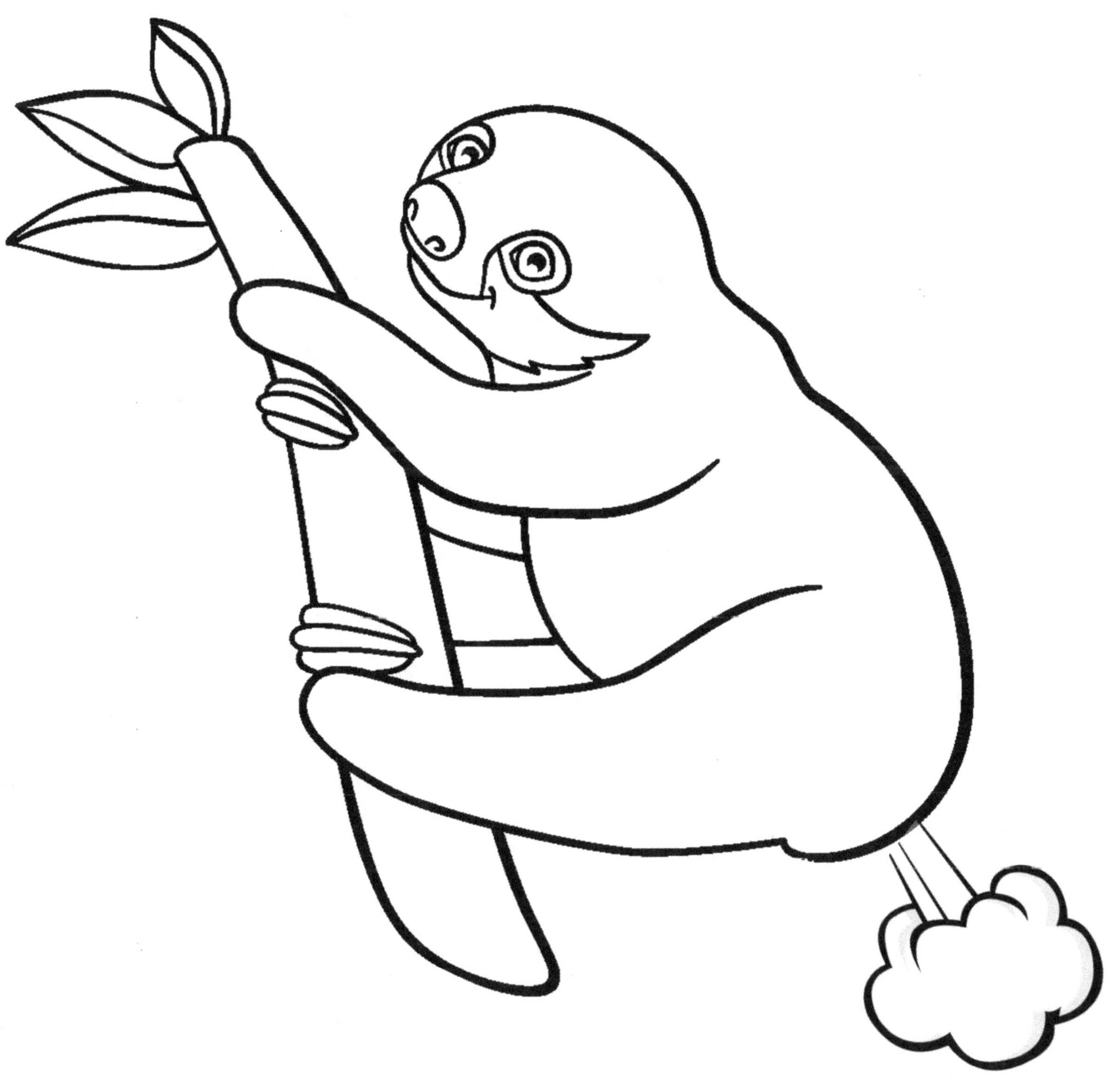

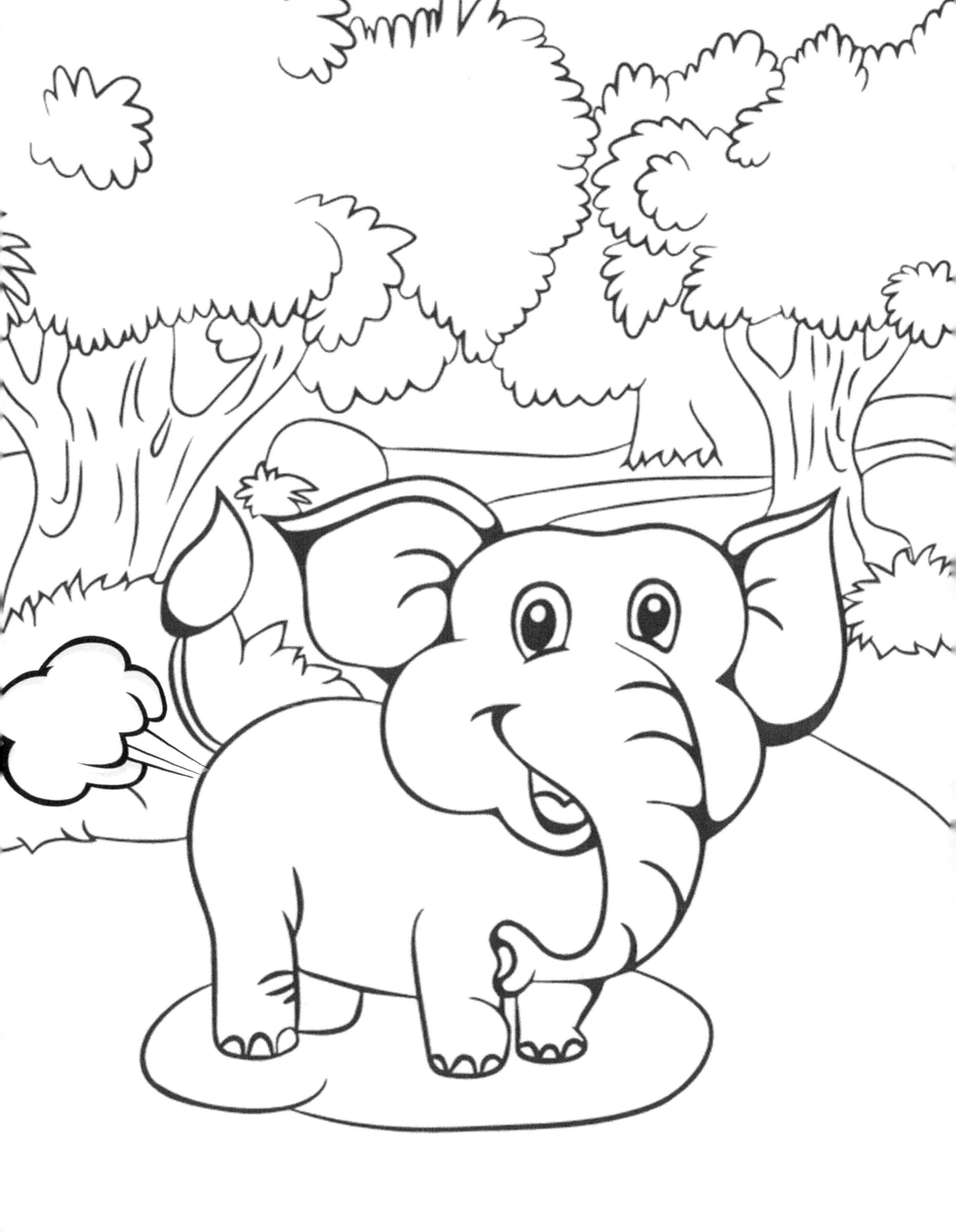

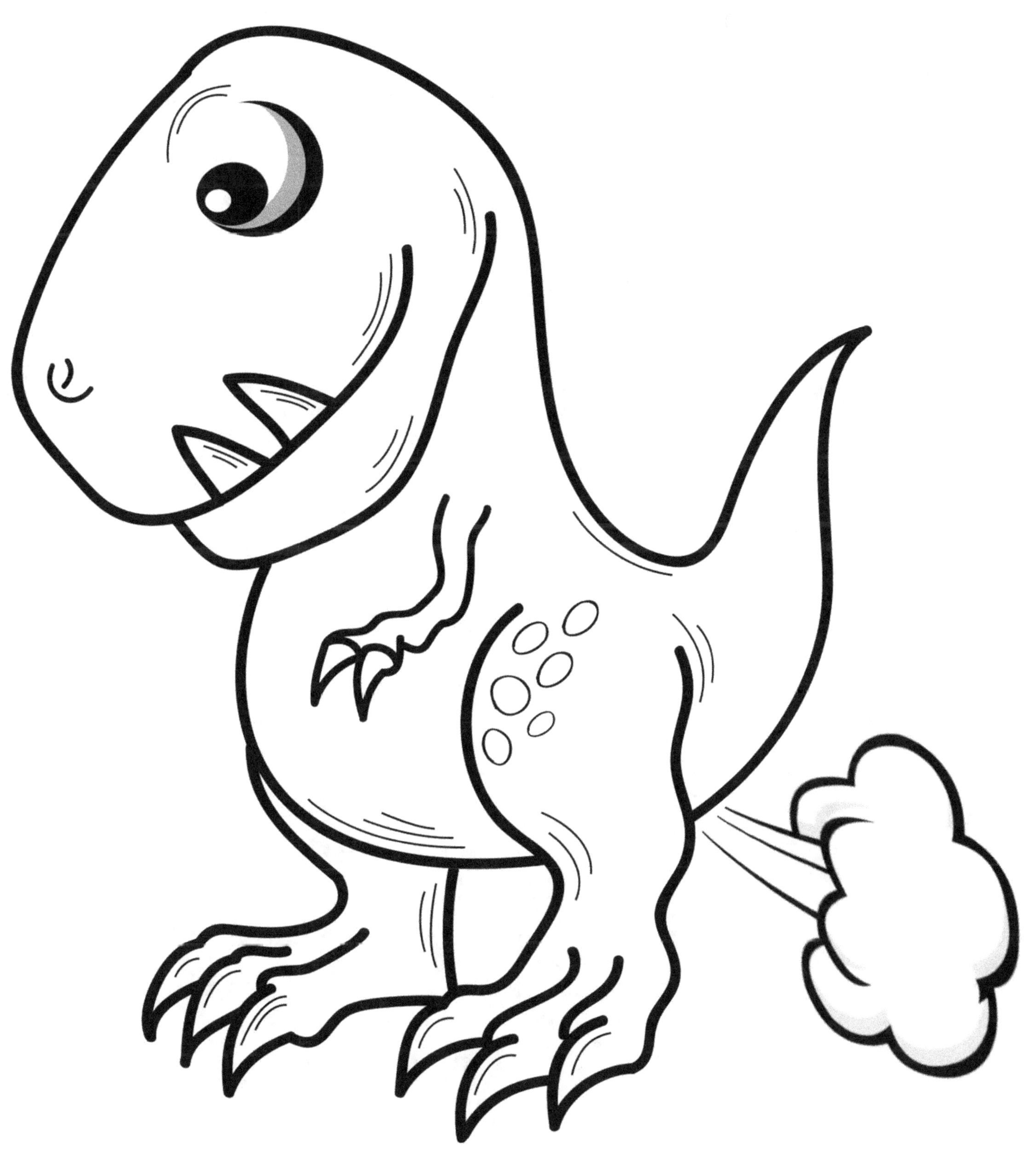

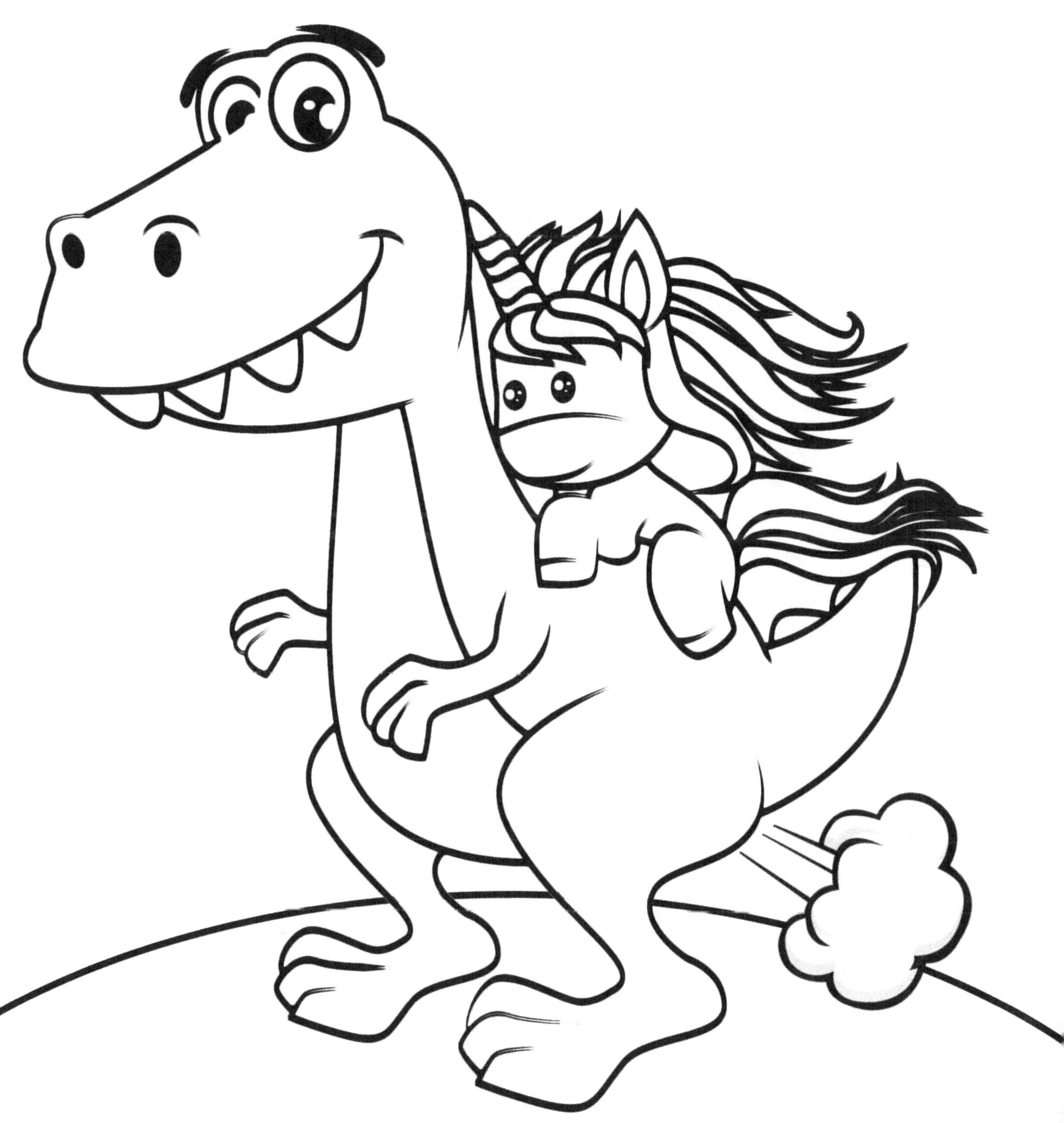

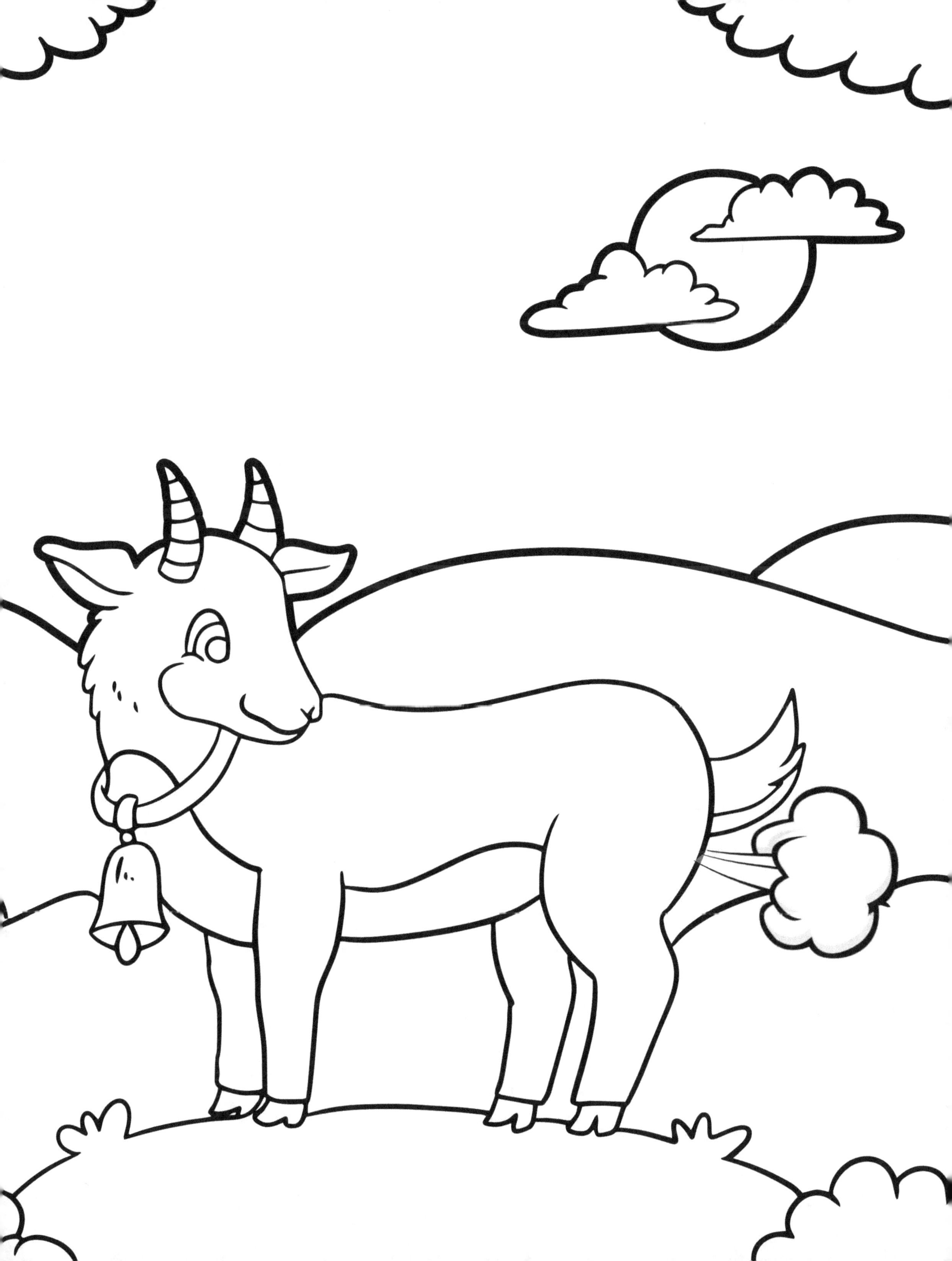

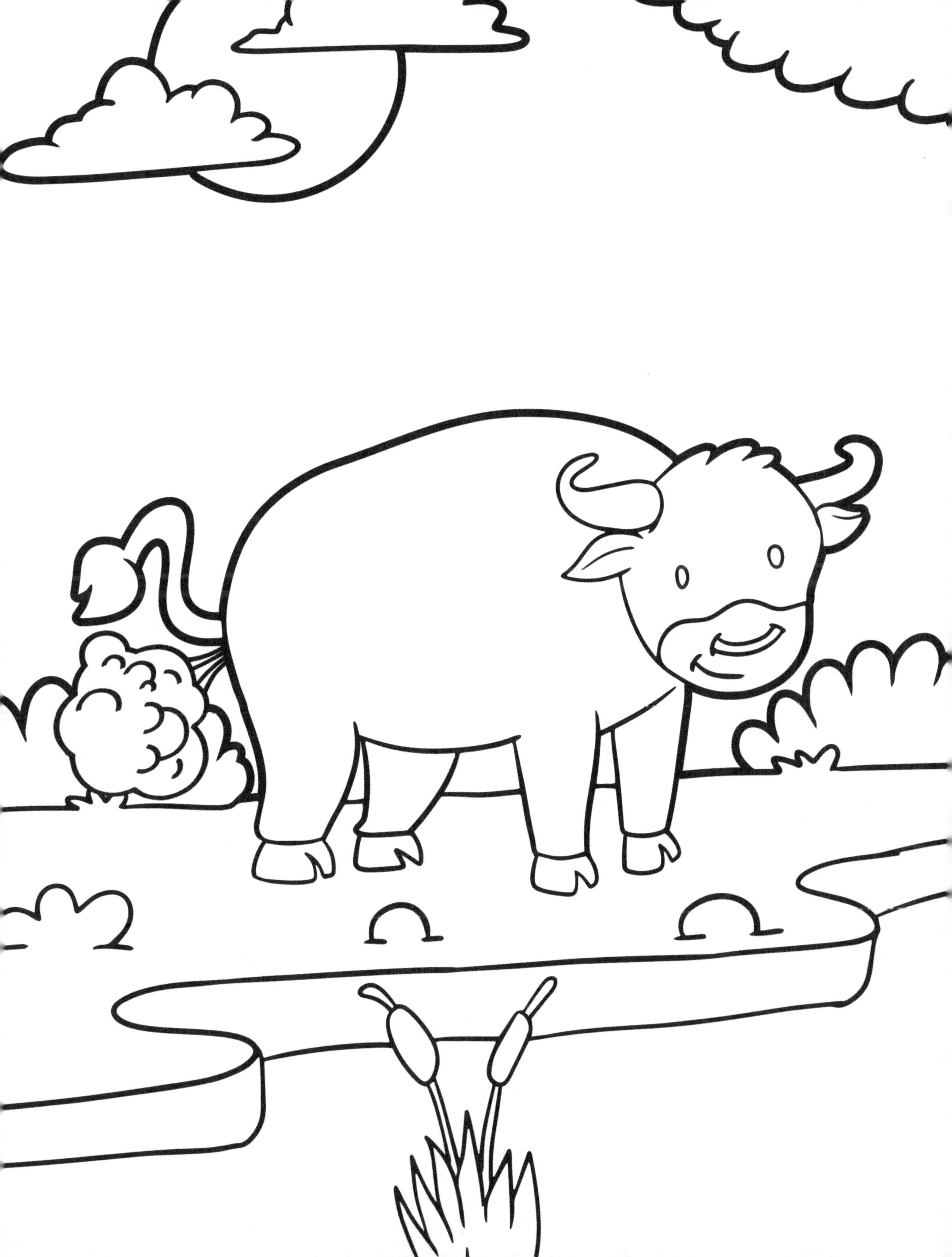

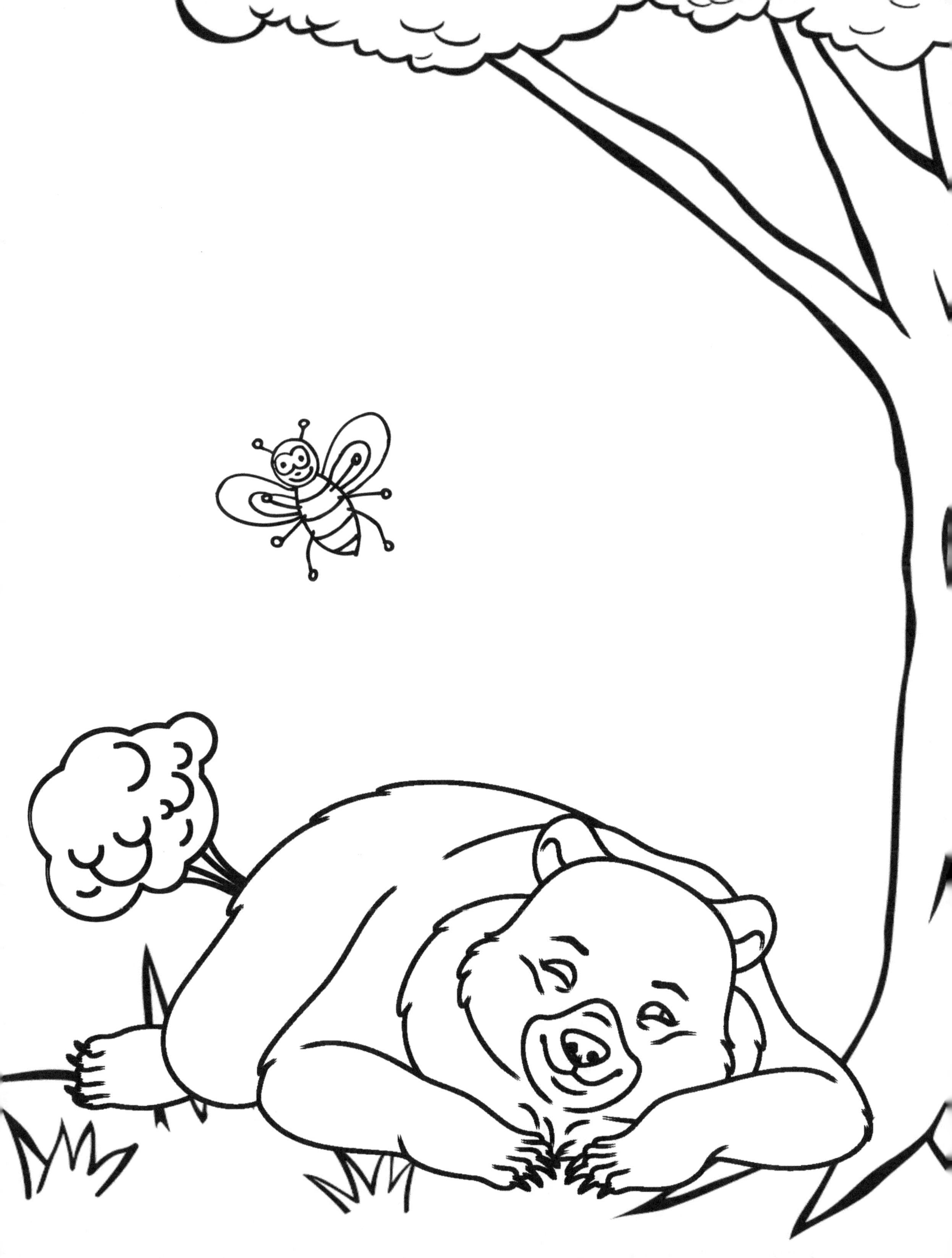

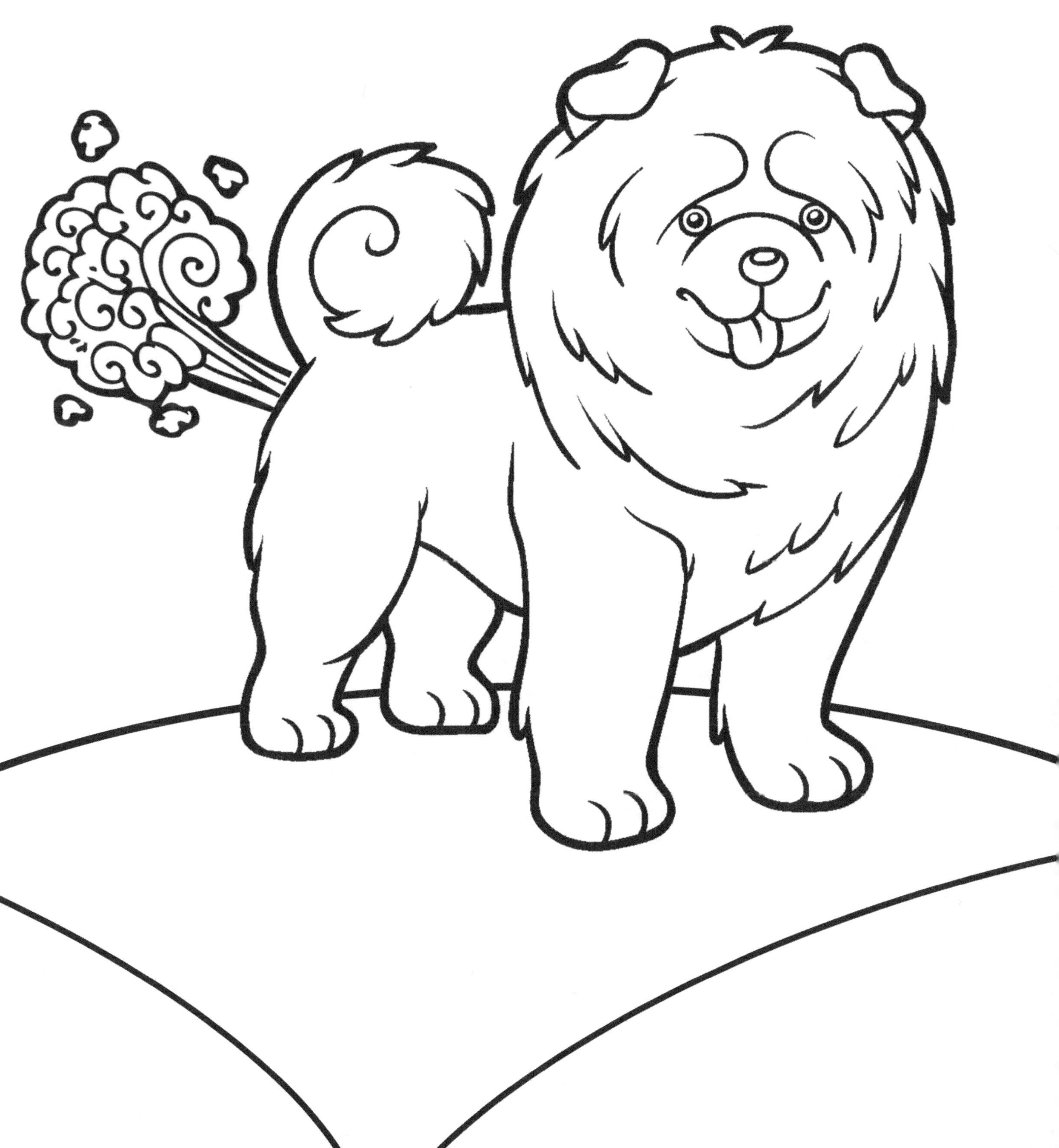

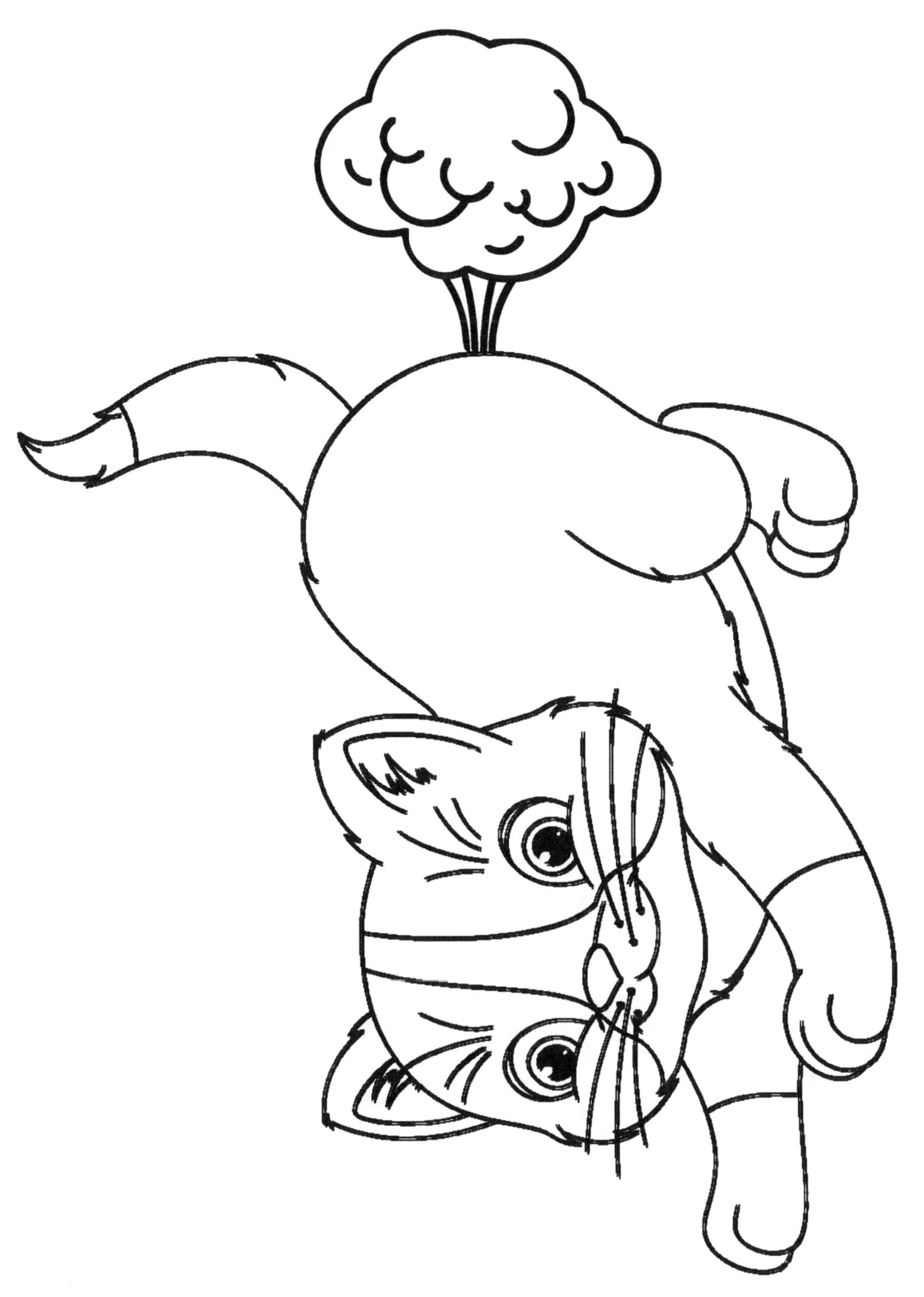

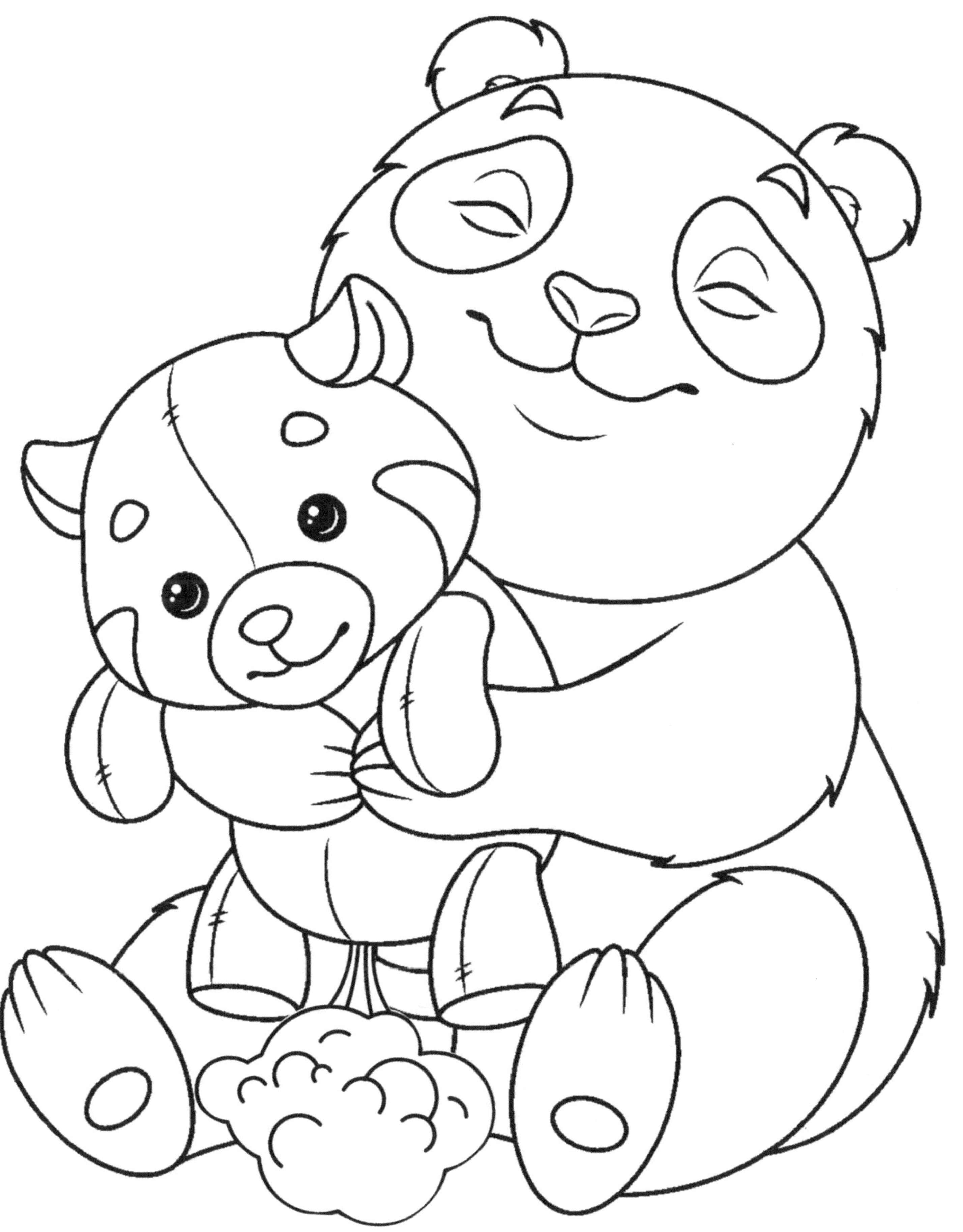

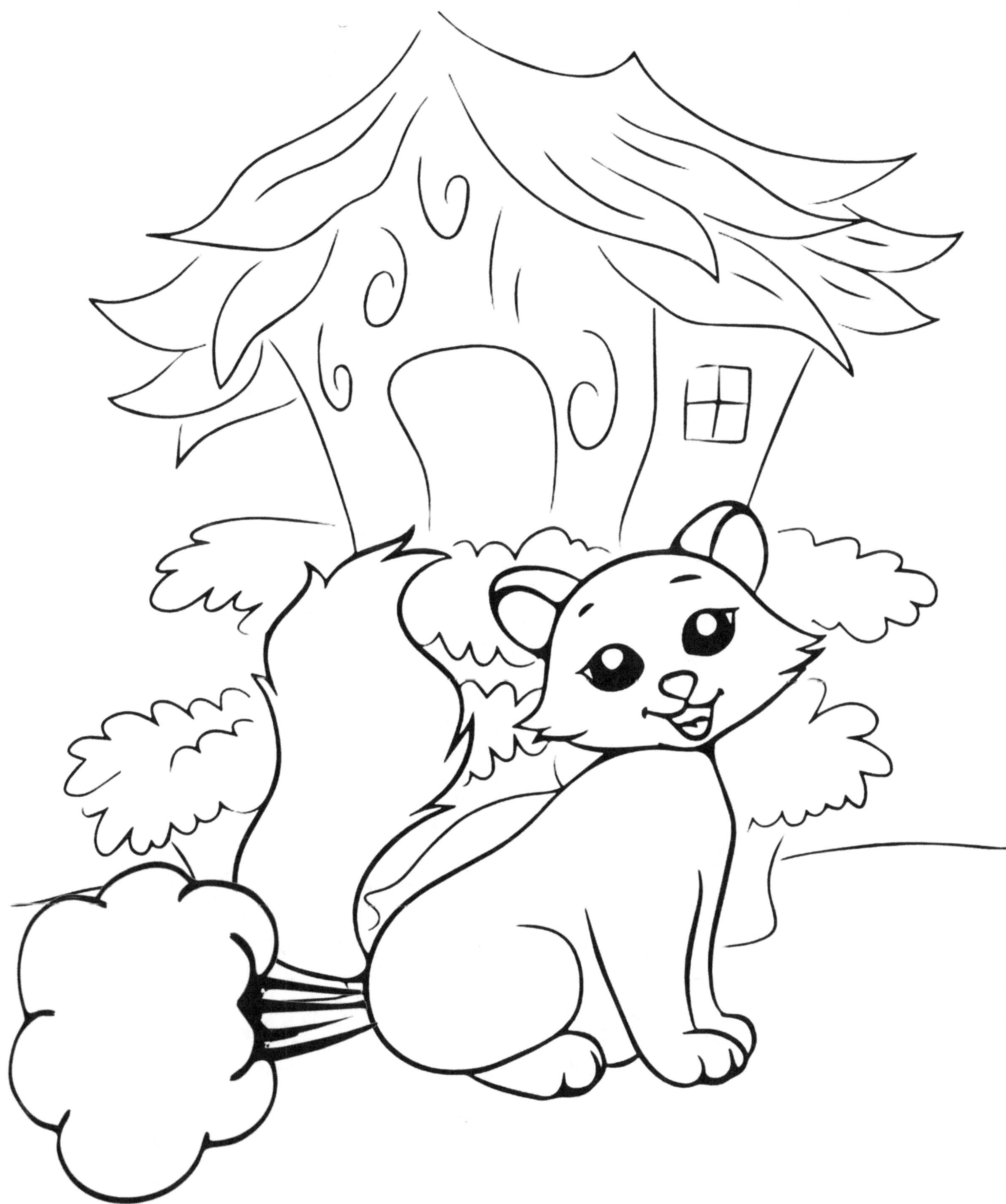

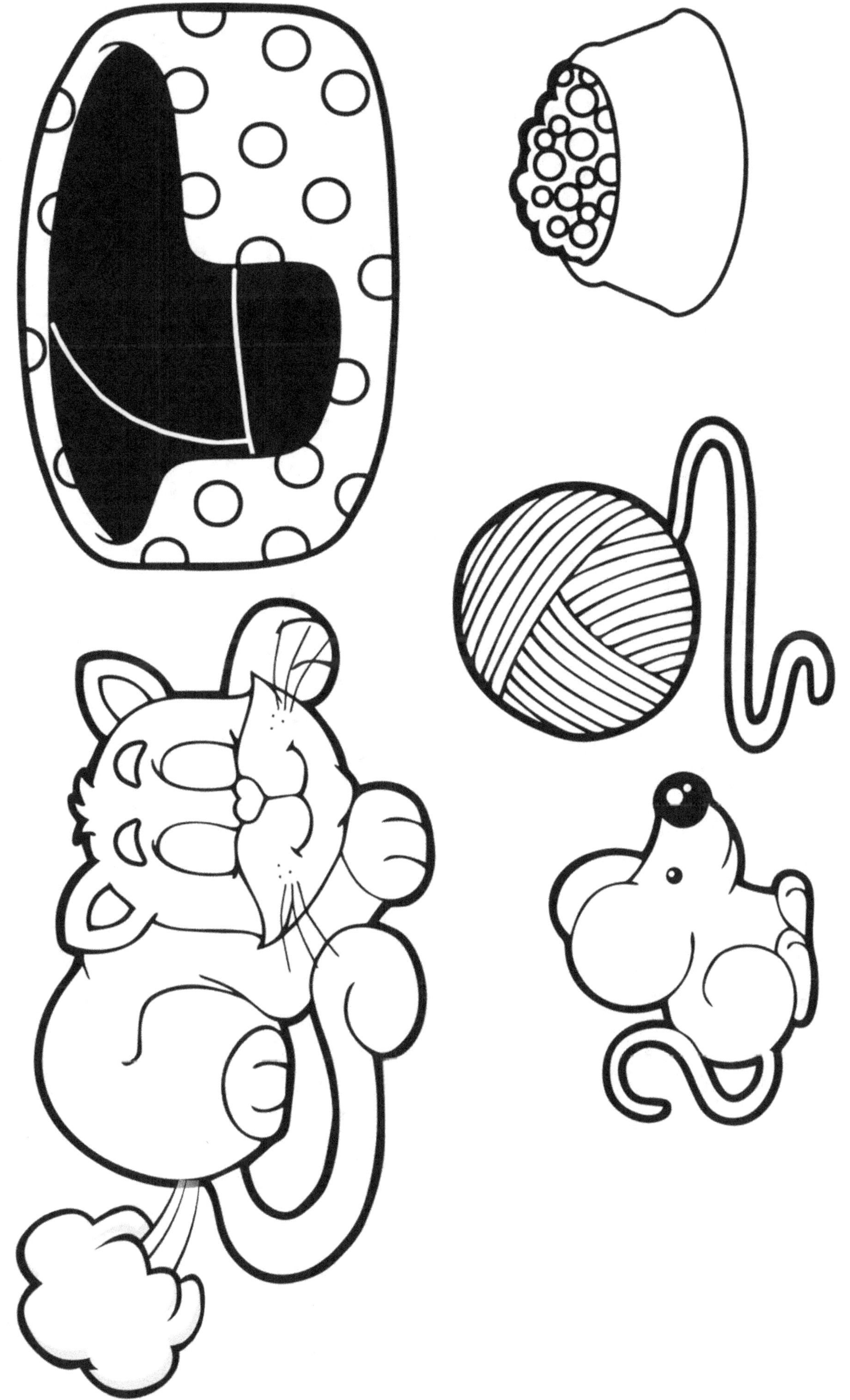

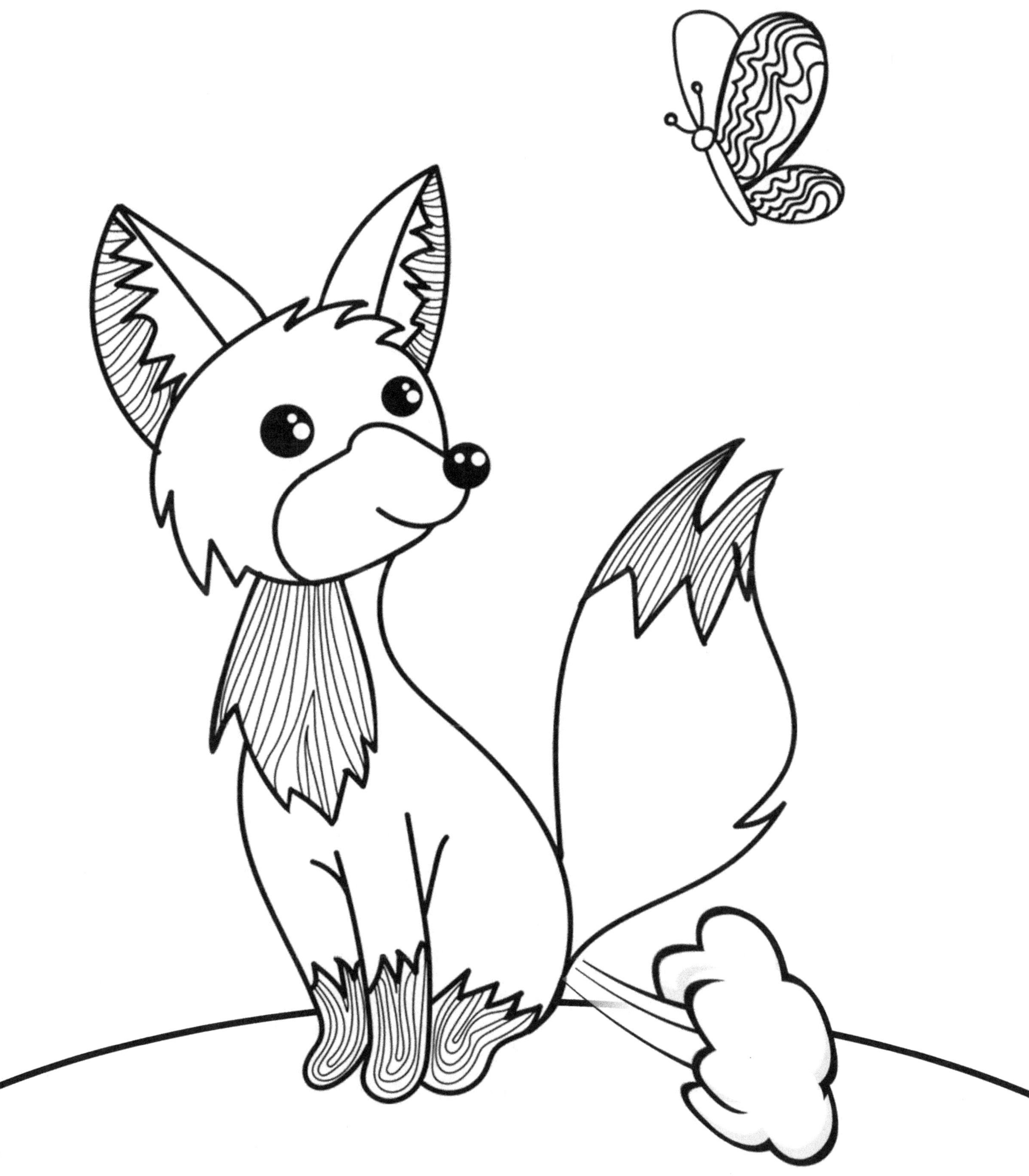

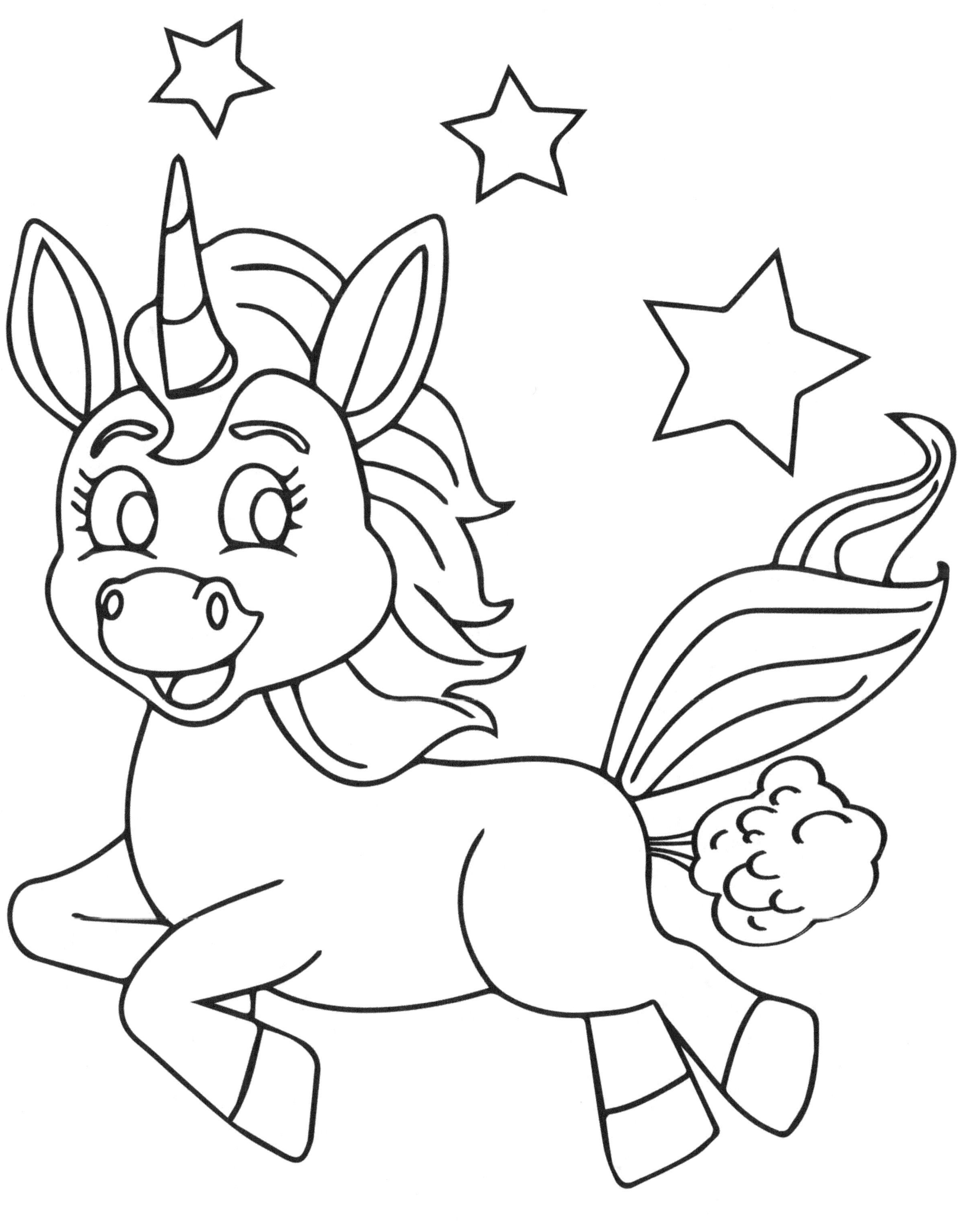

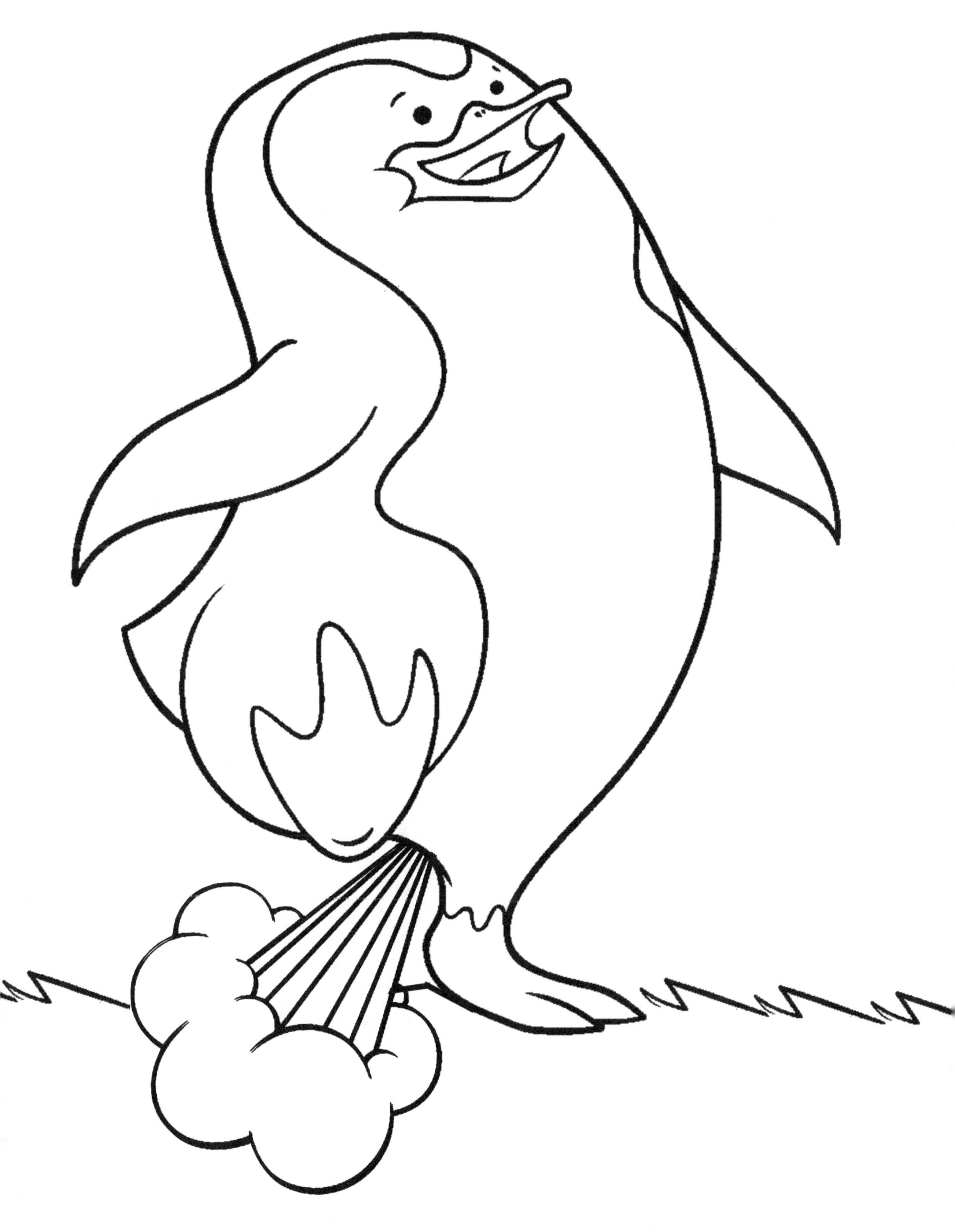

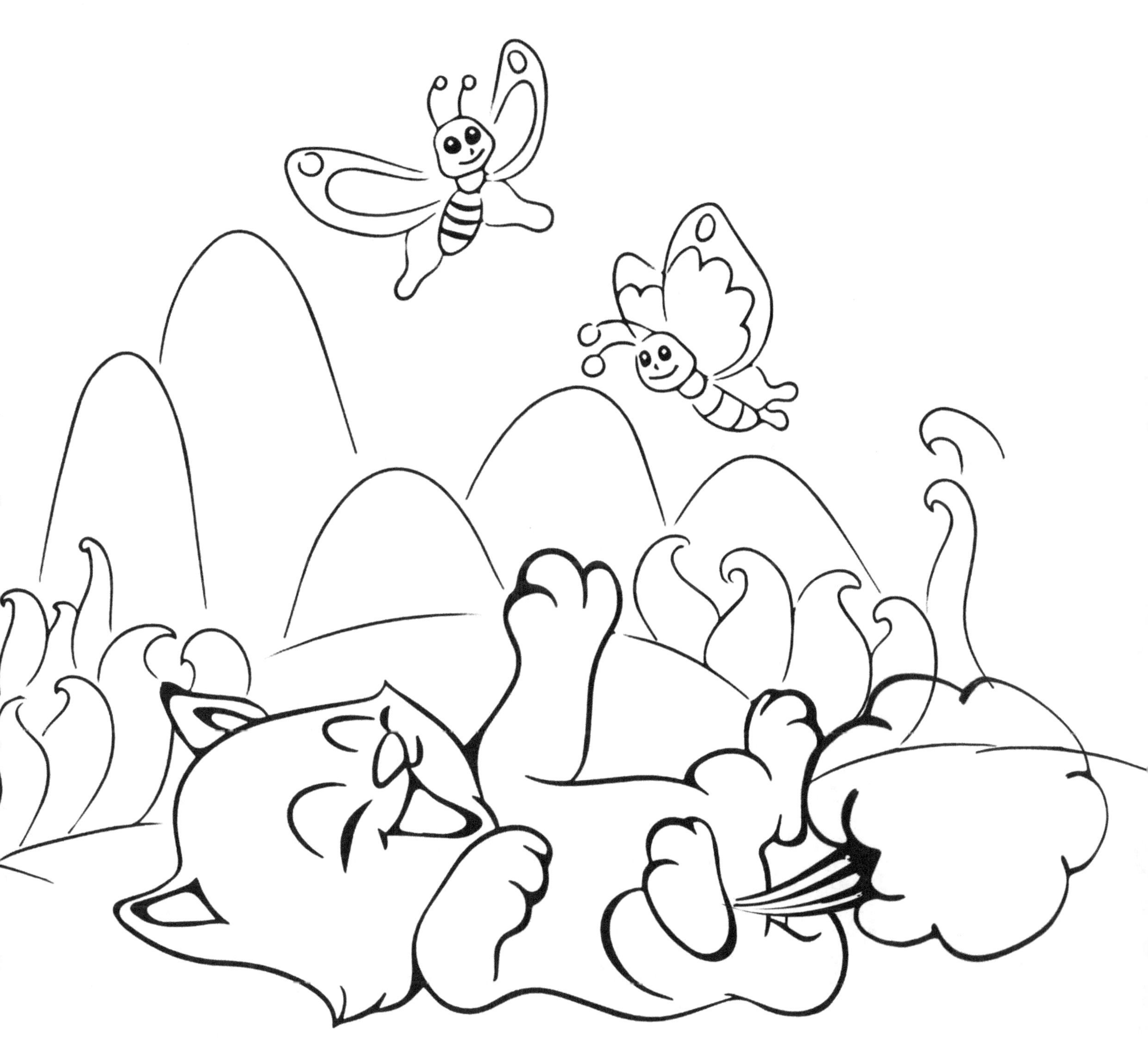

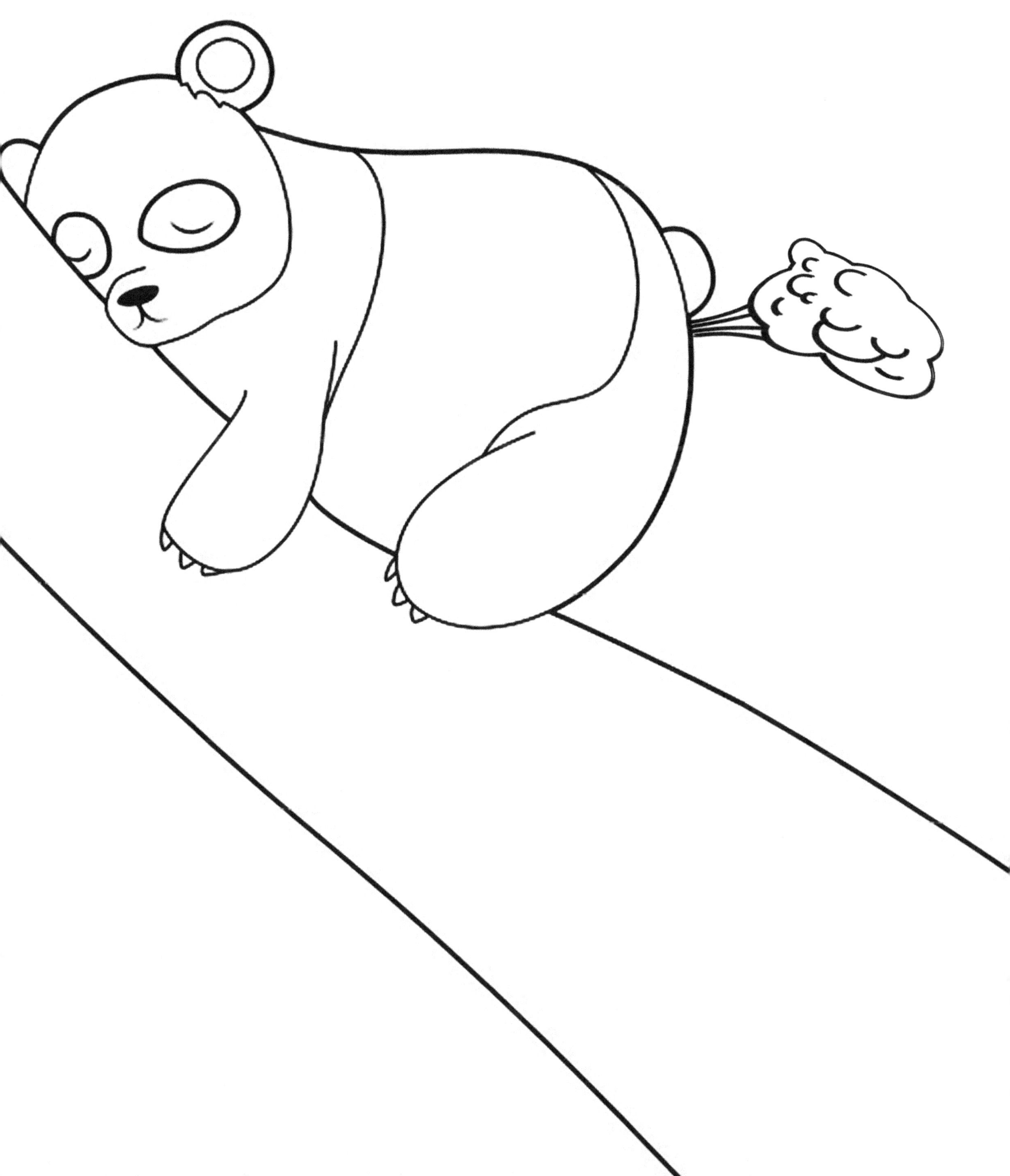

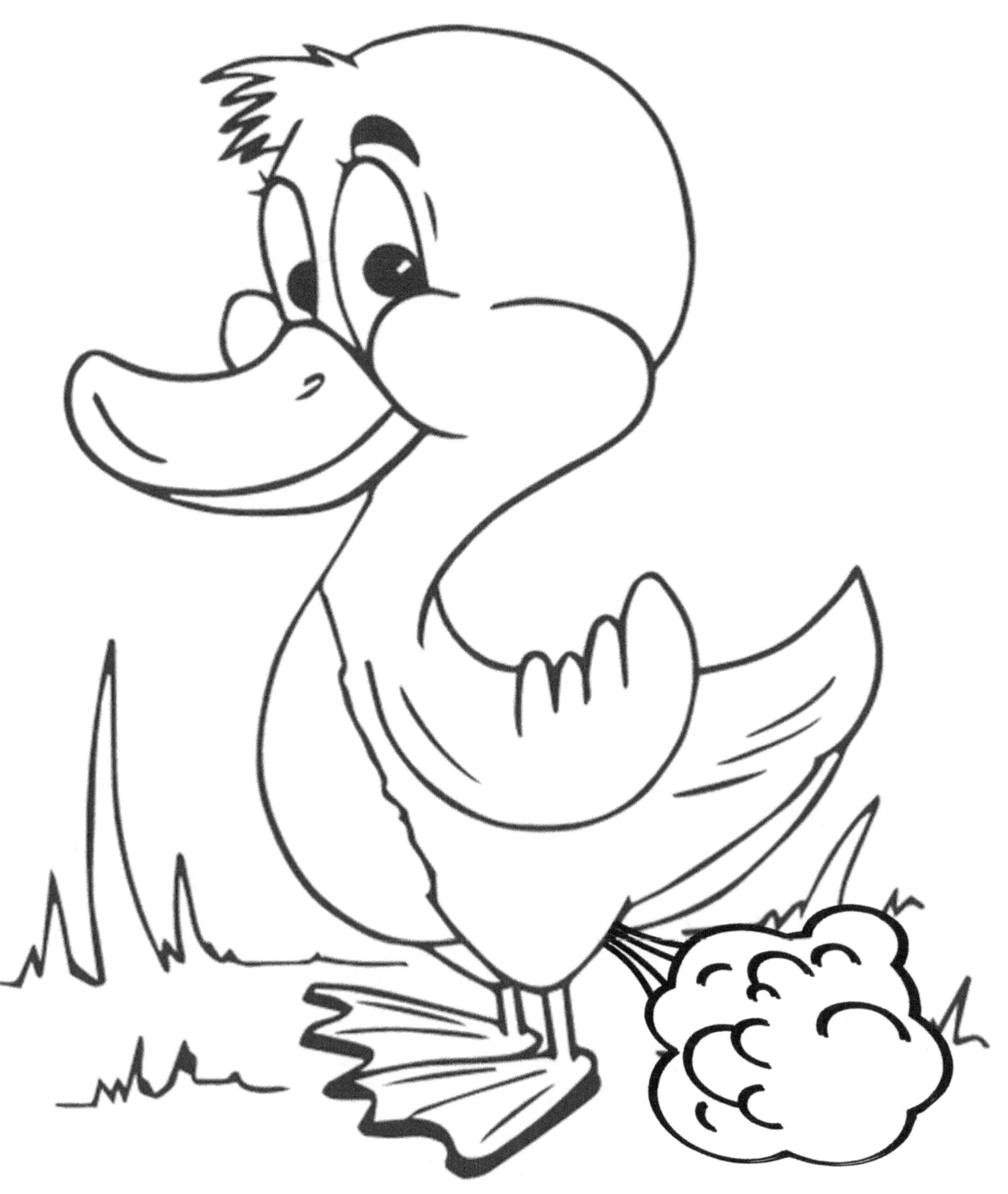

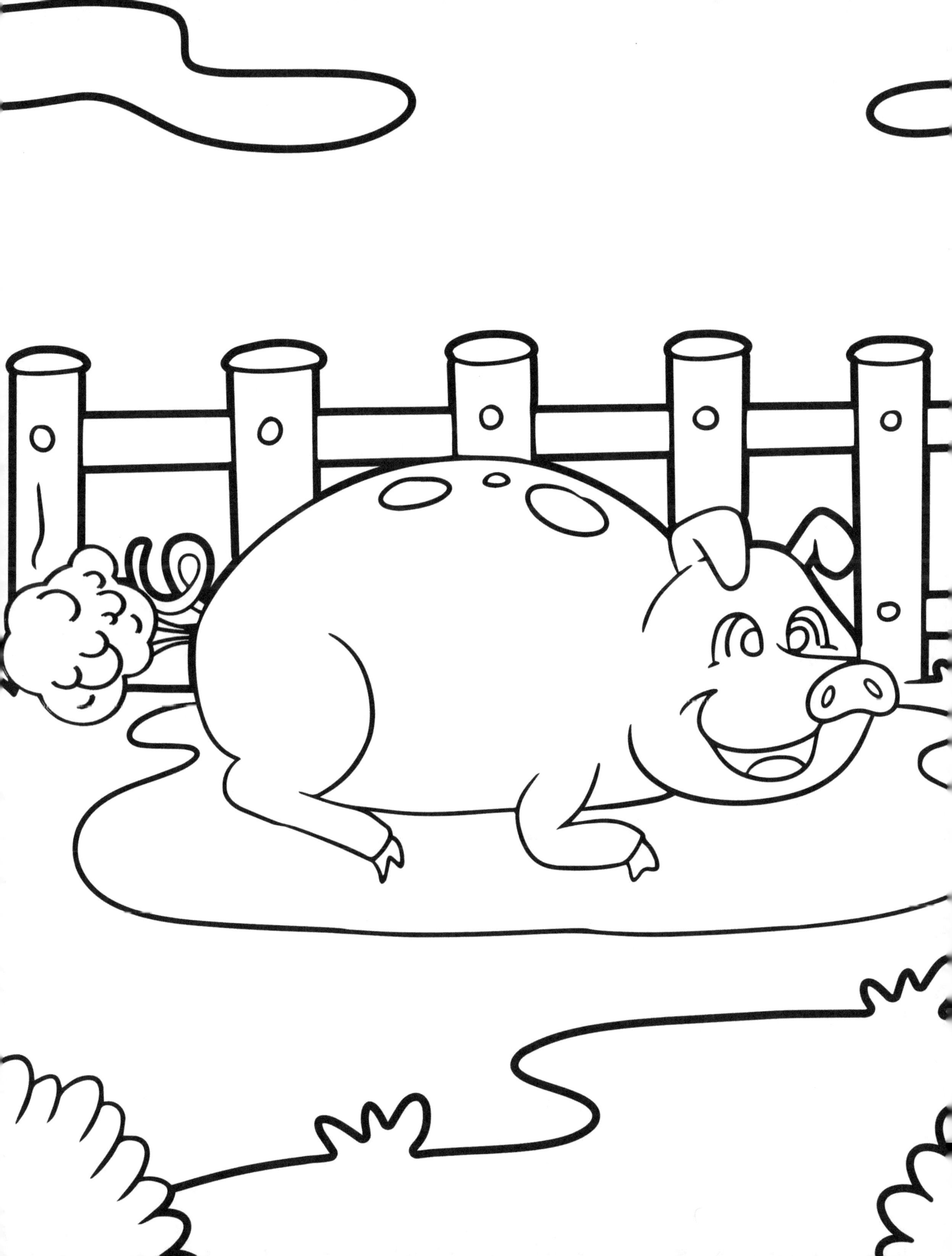

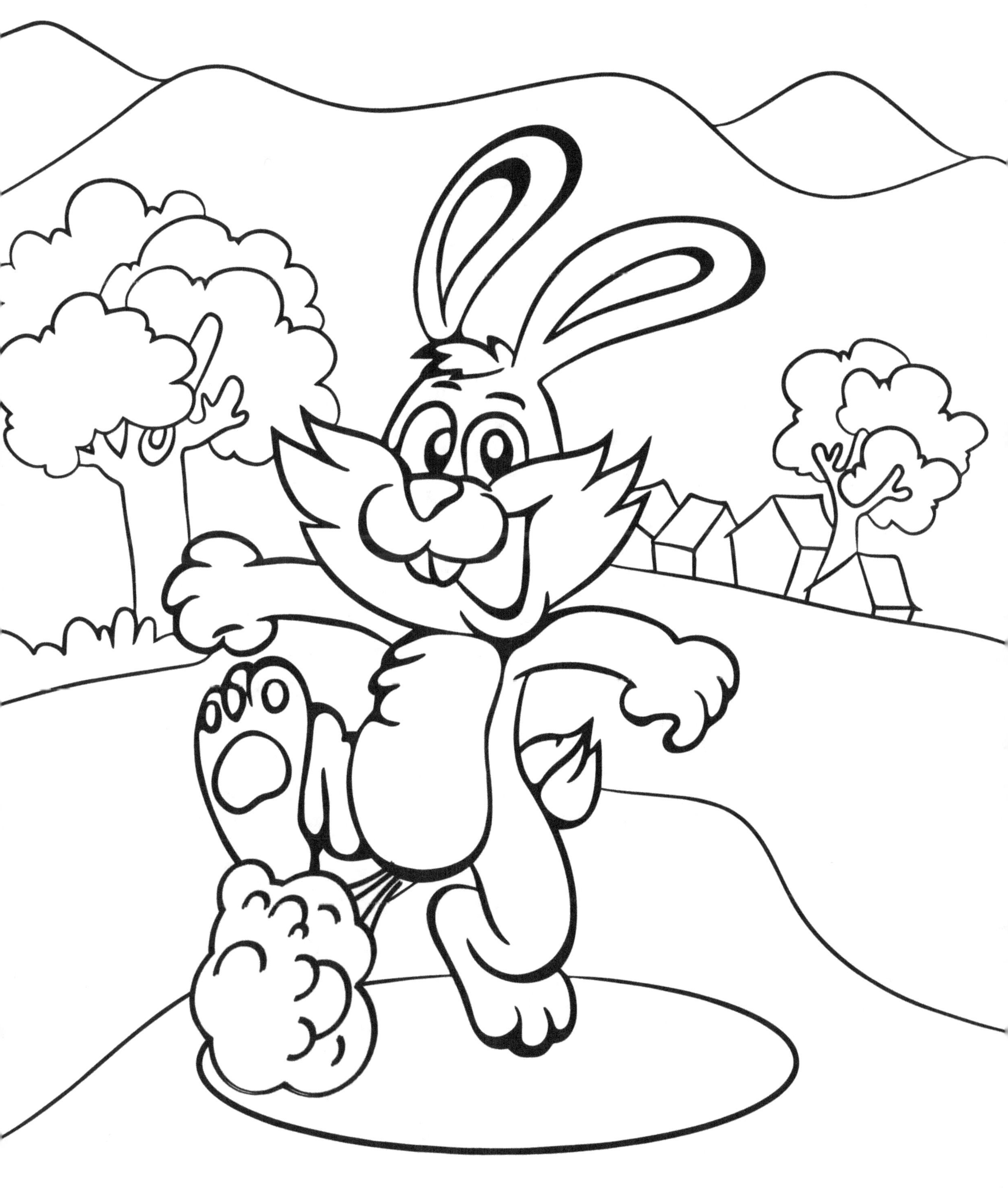

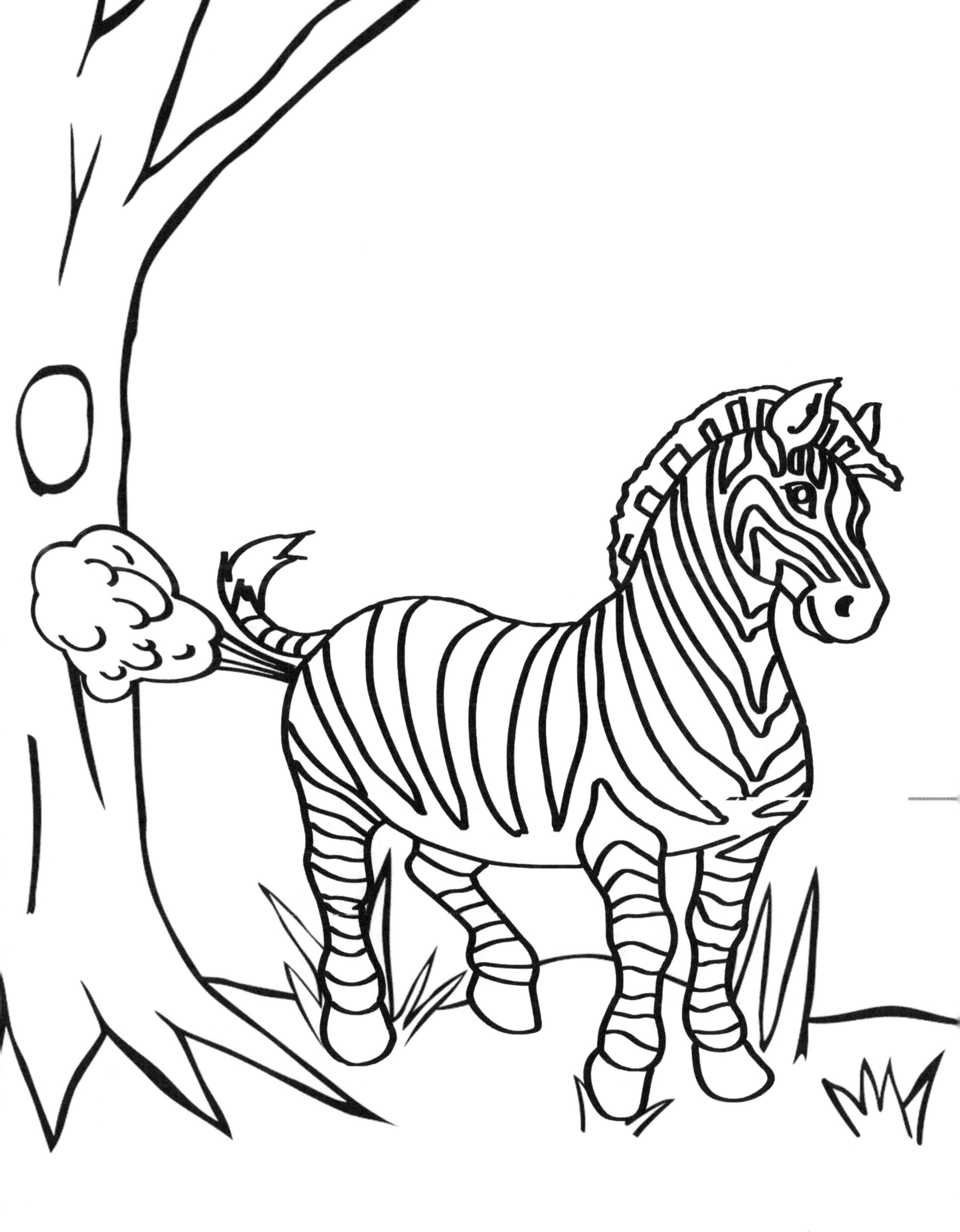

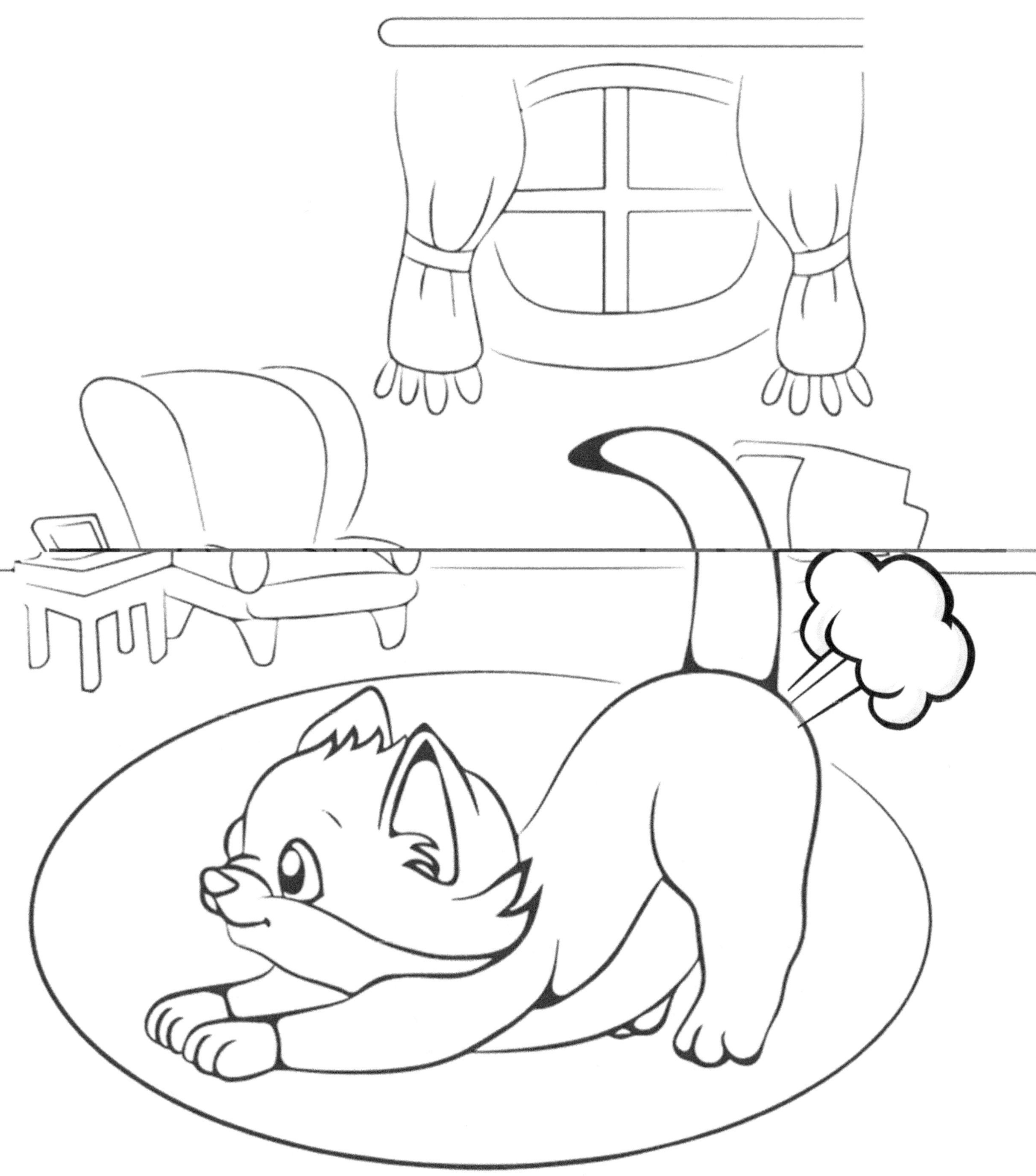

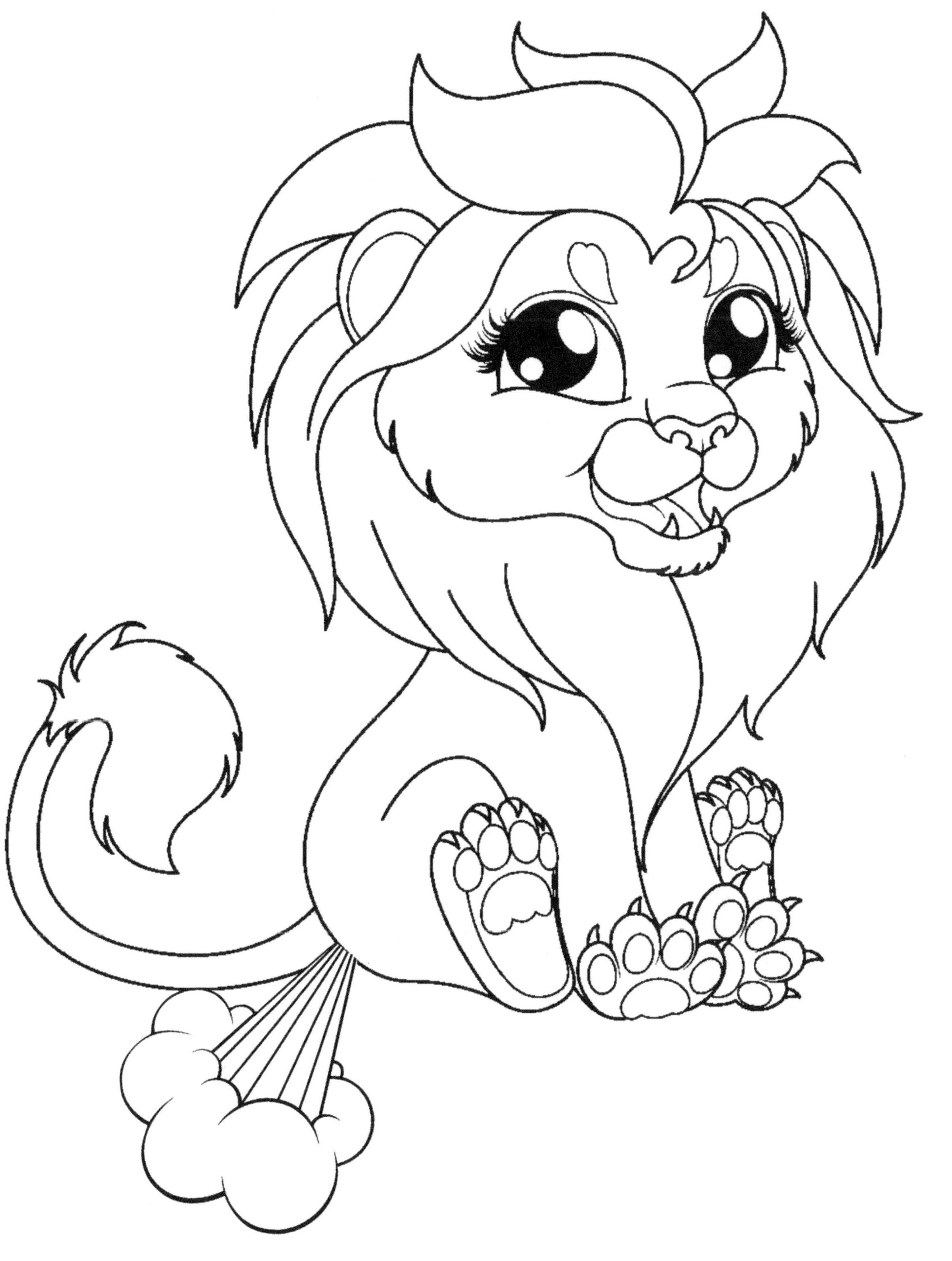

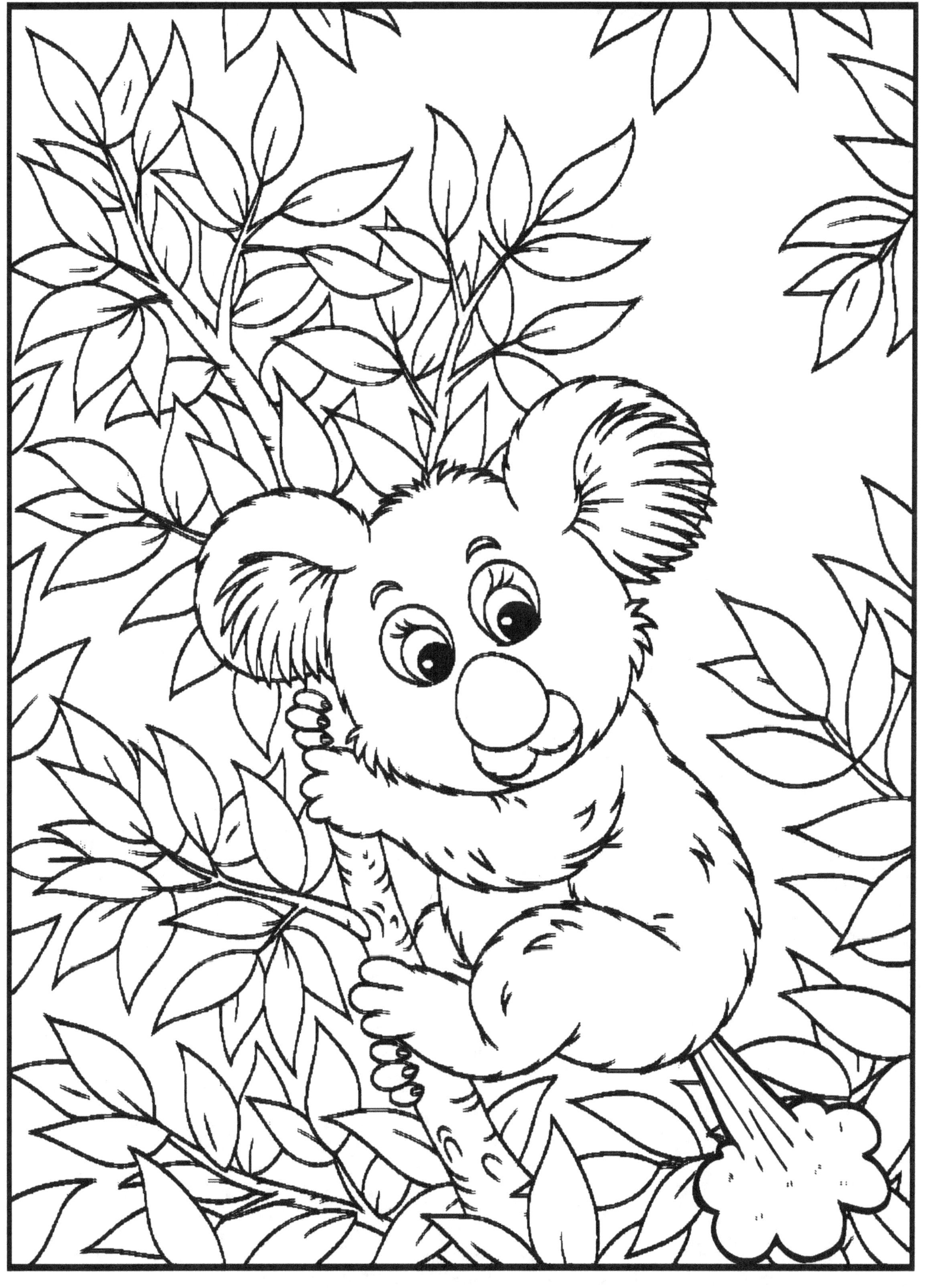

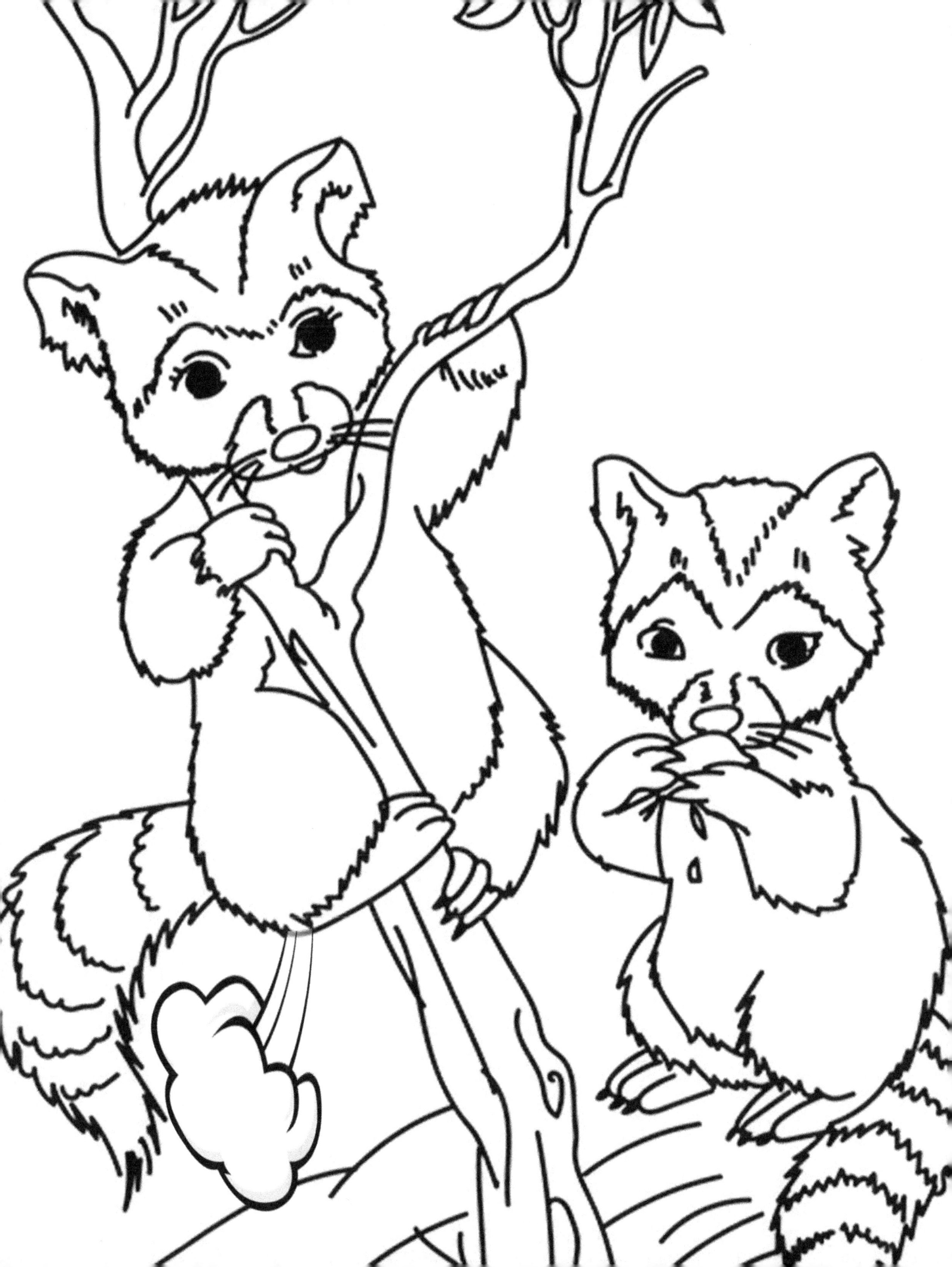

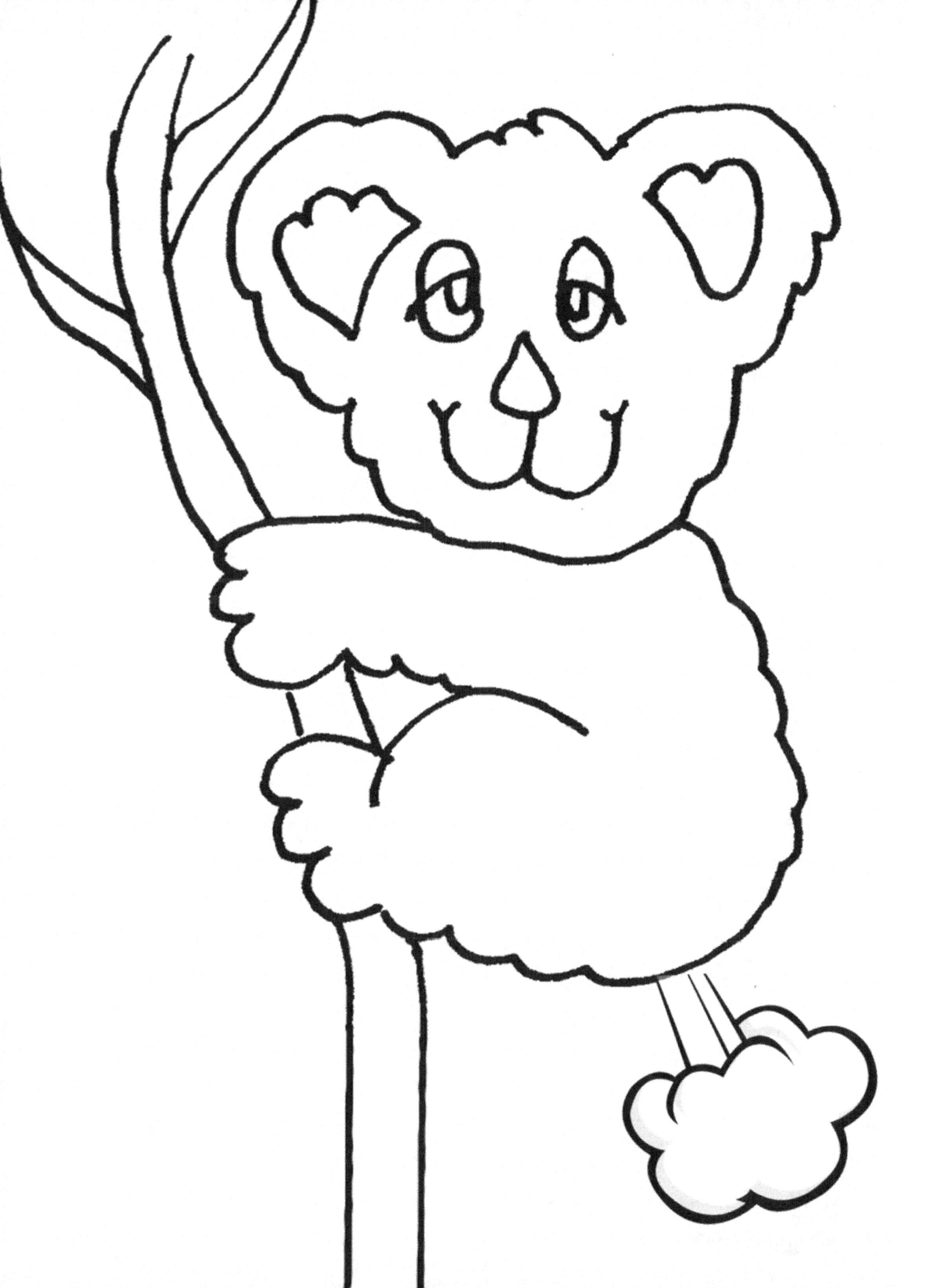